mountain bike rides

in & around

The Chilterns

ROUGH RIDE GUIDE

First published in 2007 by:

Rough Ride Guide Ltd
Walnut Tree Offices
The Old Road
Pishill
Henley-on-Thames
Oxon
RG9 6HS

ISBN 978-0-9548829-3-8

Printed by
Stephens & George Print Group
in the UK

The maps in this book have been reproduced by permission of Ordnance Survey on behalf of the Controller of Her Majesty's Stationery Office, © Crown Copyright 100037674.

DISCLAIMER

Mountain biking is a dangerous and addictive sport. The authors and publishers take no responsibility for accident, injury, death, loss of friends, or inconvenience sustained by any user of this guide as a result of information or advice contained within this guide.

This book provides information on routes with a personal insight, but is not necessarily proof of the existence of a right of way, and does not guarantee the safety and well being of any user using the information or advice contained in this guide.

Ride safely, within your limits and wear a helmet. RRG accepts no responsibility for any breakage to you or your bike, getting lost, injured, tired, lost, hungry, wet, grumpy, sunburnt, cold, or lost.

mountain bike rides in & around **The Chilterns**

SPECIAL THANKS TO:

My wife Sarah who has inspired
and supported me throughout.

My mum for helping finance it.

Friends & family for their help
and support.

The riders, clubs and bike shops
who have shared with us, their
favourite trails.

You for buying this book - I
hope you have some great rides.

EDITORS
Max Darkins
Richard Sanders

DESIGNERS
Kate Lester
Lee Bainbrigge

PHOTOGRAPHS
Max Darkins
Richard Sanders
Sarah Darkins
Ken Williams
Specialized

TECHNICAL STUFF
Ken Williams aka Mr Grey

foreword by the author

Since the release of the first A4 Rough Ride Guide books we've been lucky to have received lots of really positive feedback from riders. It also made us aware of the need for a smaller, cheaper version of the book - same concept and quality, but not such a big cash outlay. With the option to 'mix n match' further sections into your book through our website, we feel that we have come up with a truly unique product that we hope you enjoy using as much as we did making it.

Having grown up in the Chilterns it remains a special place to ride in for me - twisty, single track though beech woods, fantastic pubs, awesome wildlife and beautiful views. Furthermore, because the riding gets more technical the faster you ride, it remains an area suitable for any rider.

In these A5 guidebooks we've tried to provide information on nearby train stations and how to get to the start of the ride. If trains really aren't feasible, try to share lifts, its far more sociable and an easy way to reduce your collective carbon footprint.

Whether you're simply searching for more local rides or are using this book as a guide on your holiday, I hope that you have some great rides and new experiences, and don't stop telling us what you think.

We now have a 'notice board' on our website which we will use to provide up-to-date news and information on the routes e.g. conditions, changes, etc. The success of this 'notice board' will rely heavily on your input, so please e-mail us with any news and information you have.

Mountain bikers are generally a friendly bunch, who will stop and chat, admire each others bikes and assist with breakdowns, so lets keep it that way. It is a sport that anyone can enjoy, so make the effort to make everyone feel welcome, whatever their age, sex or ability.

Happy riding.

Max Darkins

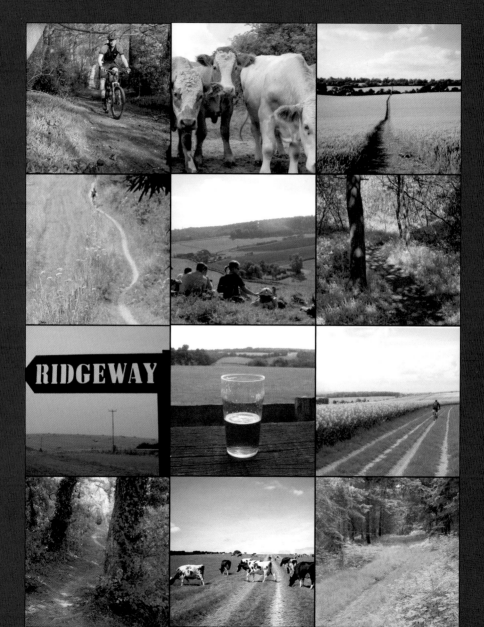

RIDGEWAY

INTRODUCTION

The Rough Ride Guide books are designed to let *you* choose which sections you would like to have in your book. The standard book has a selection of routes, to which you can add more routes and further supplements, such as our maintenance & repair manual. These can all be purchased from our website www.roughrideguide.co.uk.

TOP TIP: We advice all riders, especially new comers to the sport, to get the 'Introduction to mountain biking' as it has lots of useful information and tips, to enable you to get and make the most of the sport, and gain maximum enjoyment.

THE ROUTE GRADING

Please bear in mind that peoples opinions vary, as well as their speed and line choice, which all play a big factor in determining the difficulty level of a route. Grading our routes is also made more difficult by the fact that our routes usually have shortcut and extension options, which is why our routes usually have a grading between 2 levels.

We have graded our the routes from Easy to Extreme, bearing in mind the terrain, distance, height gained, and opportunity to bail-out, or be rescued should naything go wrong.

Also, to keep some consistency and familiarity to grading trails, we have adopted the ratings and colour coding used by various parties, including the Forestry Commission (but our yellow is their green).

EASY (YELLOW): Suitable for beginners. Generally wide, well surfaced, easy going tracks.

MEDIUM (BLUE): Suitable for intermediate riders. Rougher terrain, single track, requires a choice of line and some technical ability.

HARD (RED): Suitable for experienced riders only. Good bike control required, quick decision making, and some healthy lungs.

EXTREME (BLACK): Suitable for very experienced and competent riders. Contains some very technical and potentially dangerous terrain.

COUNTRYSIDE CODE

Only ride on open trails
Be in control of your bike at all times
Slow down or stop and let people pass by
Warn people of your presence by calling or ringing a bell, pass slowly and be polite
Don't scare any animals
Don't leave any rubbish
Look ahead and be aware
Be kind & courteous to other trail users
Shut gates behind you

TOP TIP: Fix a bell to your bike to politely warn others of your presence - it has even been known to raise a smile from walkers.

BLOCKED TRAILS
There are a couple of very useful websites provided by the CTC that enable you to report / enter the details of a blocked Right of Way e.g. a locked gate at www.clearthattrail.org.uk or for pot holes in roads (a big cause of cycling accidents) at www.fillthathole.org.uk.

• **NOTE**: You are perfectly within your rights to continue along the path (or where it should be), by passing around or climbing over the obstacle.

• **NOTE**: If an aggressive animal e.g. a dog is stopping you from progressing on a public ROW, inform the police.

USING ROUGH RIDE GUIDE MAPS

Our aim when producing these guidebooks has been to offer clear, fun and challenging routes, suitable for all abilities. To achieve this we have used the best mapping, sought local riders knowledge, and provided shortcut and extension options. This will ensure that everyone can find and ride the best trails, with minimum effort and hassle.

▪ **NOTE:** We have made every effort to ensure that these routes only use legal paths, but access rights can change or mistakes be made, so if you are ever unsure, please walk your bike to avoid confrontation.

(RRG) ABBREVIATIONS

To reduce the amount of text you have to read through, we have abbreviated the frequently used words. It looks a long list, but most are obvious.

L = Left
R = Right
SA = Straight ahead / across
Bear = A bend of less than 90 degrees
T-J = T-Junction (usually at 180 degrees)
Fork = Track splits into two directions
X-rds = Cross roads (4 road junction)
X-tracks = As X-rds, but tracks not roads
DH = Downhill
UH = Uphill
FP = Footpath
BW = Bridleway
ByW = By-Way
(P)ROW = (Public) Right of way
RUPP = Road used as public path
BOAT = By-way open to all traffic
DT = Double track (wide enough for a car)
ST = Single track (narrow trail).

▪ **NOTE:** Emboldened directions provide the 'must know' information, and the other directions provide greater detail for when you may be unsure.

DISTANCE

The (blue) main route is usually around 30 kilometres / 20 miles, which will be suitable for most competent and fit mountain bikers, with (yellow) shortcut and (red) extension options for riders wanting to adjust the length to suit their needs.

HEIGHT

The main route shows the distance and amount of climbing. The extension or shortcut will have a + or - figure, to show the change in distance and climbing from the main route. For example, if the main route is 30 kilometres with 500 metres of climbing, and you ride this and the extension which reads +7 kilometress and +150 meters of climbing, you will ride a total of 37 kilometres with 650 metres of climbing.

TOP TIP: A bike computer is very useful to show you exactly how far you have gone, so you can follow the distances we provide between points. Discrepancies do occur, so use them as a guide, not gospel.

▪ **NOTE:** The amount of climbing involved on the route is just as important as the distance. Generally, 300+ meters of climbing over 10 miles is strenuous, so any ride of 30 miles with over 900 meters of climbing is going to be very tough. See the route profile below.

We have provided distances in both kilometres, and miles (in brackets), as although we are starting to become familiar with KM, most of us have grown up using and thinking in miles.

ROUTE PROFILE

These are at the bottom of the route directions, showing you the cross section / height gained and lost, on the main route. The numbers above the profile correlate to the route text numbering.

ORDNANCE SURVEY (LANDRANGER) MAP KEY

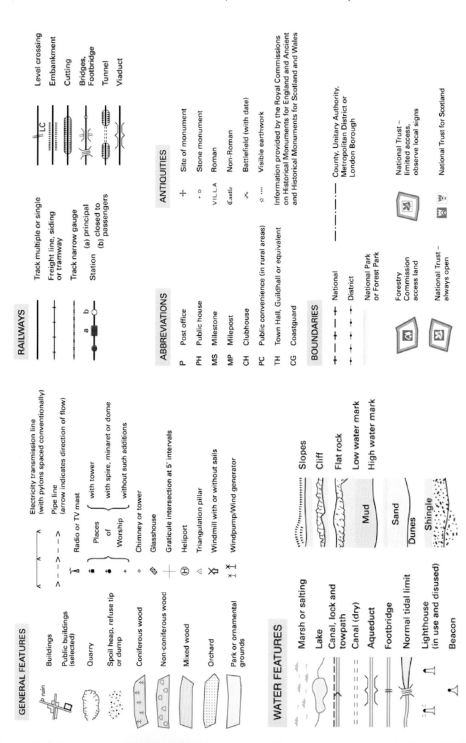

GENERAL FEATURES

Buildings

Public buildings (selected)

Quarry

Spoil heap, refuse tip or dump

Coniferous wood

Non-coniferous wood

Mixed wood

Orchard

Park or ornamental grounds

Electricity transmission line (with pylons spaced conventionally)

Pipe line (arrow indicates direction of flow)

Radio or TV mast

Places of Worship — with tower / with spire, minaret or dome / without such additions

Chimney or tower

Glasshouse

Graticule intersection at 5′ intervals

Heliport

Triangulation pillar

Windmill with or without sails

Windpump/Wind generator

WATER FEATURES

Marsh or salting

Lake

Canal, lock and towpath

Canal (dry)

Aqueduct

Footbridge

Normal tidal limit

Lighthouse (in use and disused)

Beacon

Slopes

Cliff

Flat rock

Low water mark

High water mark

Mud

Sand

Dunes

Shingle

RAILWAYS

Track multiple or single

Freight line, siding or tramway

Track narrow gauge

Station (a) principal (b) closed to passengers

Level crossing

Embankment

Cutting

Bridges, Footbridge

Tunnel

Viaduct

ABBREVIATIONS

P   Post office

PH   Public house

MS   Milestone

MP   Milepost

CH   Clubhouse

PC   Public convenience (in rural areas)

TH   Town Hall, Guildhall or equivalent

CG   Coastguard

ANTIQUITIES

+   Site of monument

· o Stone monument

VILLA Roman

Castle Non-Roman

⚔   Battlefield (with date)

☆ ⸬ Visible earthwork

Information provided by the Royal Commissions on Historical Monuments for England and Ancient and Historical Monuments for Scotland and Wales

BOUNDARIES

National

District

National Park or Forest Park

County, Unitary Authority, Metropolitan District or London Borough

Forestry Commission access land

National Trust – always open

National Trust – limited access, observe local signs

National Trust for Scotland

ORDNANCE SURVEY (LANDRANGER) MAP KEY

ROADS AND PATHS

Not necessarily rights of way

Service area M1	Junction number 3
	Elevated
Unfenced	Motorway (dual carriageway)
A 470 (T)	Motorway under construction
A 493	Footbridge
	Dual carriageway
B 4518	Trunk road
A 855	Main road
	Main road under construction
	Secondary road
Bridge B 885	Narrow road with passing places
Ferry P	Road generally more than 4 m wide
Ferry V	Road generally less than 4 m wide
	Other road, drive or track
	Path
	Gradient: steeper than 20% (1 in 5) 14% to 20% (1 in 7 to 1 in 5)
	Gates Road Tunnel
	Ferry (passenger) Ferry (vehicle)

TOURIST INFORMATION

- *i* Information centre, all year/seasonal
- Selected places of tourist interest
- Viewpoint
- P Parking
- Youth hostel
- Golf course or links
- Bus or coach station
- ⚲ Public telephone
- ⚲ Motoring organisation telephone
- PC Public convenience (in rural areas)
- Picnic site
- Camp site
- Caravan site

PUBLIC RIGHTS OF WAY

--------	Footpath
-- -- --	Bridleway
+-+-+-+	Road used as public path
+-+-+-+	Byway open to all traffic

Public rights of way shown on this map have been taken from local authority definitive maps and later amendments. The map includes changes notified to Ordnance Survey by (date). The symbols show the defined route so far as the scale of mapping will allow. Rights of way are not shown on maps of Scotland.

Rights of way are liable to change and may not be clearly defined on the ground. Please check with the relevant local authority for the latest information.

The representation on this map of any other road, track or path is no evidence of the existence of a right of way.

Danger Area   Firing and Test Ranges in the area. Danger! Observe warning notices

OTHER PUBLIC ACCESS

♦	National Trail, Long Distance Route, selected Recreational Paths
●	National/Regional Cycle Network
· · ·	Other route with public access
- - -	Surfaced cycleroute
4	National Cycle Network number
8	Regional Cycle Network number

The exact nature of the rights on these routes and the existence of any restrictions may be checked with the local highway authority. Alignments are based on the best information available. These routes are not shown on maps of Scotland.

ROCK FEATURES

outcrop   cliff   650   scree   600

HEIGHTS

50	Contours are at 10 metres vertical interval
·144	Heights are to the nearest metre above mean sea level

Heights shown close to a triangulation pillar refer to the station height at ground level and not necessarily to the summit.

1 metre = 3.2808 feet

ROUTES

ROUTES

No	NAME	GRADING	DISTANCE (KM)	+ / - (KM)	CLIMBING (METRES)
01	MARLBOROUGH NORTH	EASY / MEDIUM	25	-7.25	400
02	MARLBOROUGH SOUTH	MEDIUM	24.1	-5.2 or 6.6	380
03	WANTAGE	MEDIUM / HARD	29.5	+5 & +4.5 or -10.5	480
04	STREATLEY	MEDIUM / HARD	29	+3.2 & +10.5 or -6	495
05	BURGHCLERE	MEDIUM	27.4	+17.2	490
06	YATELEY COMMON	EASY / MEDIUM	18.5	Various	140
07	WOODCOTE NORTH	MEDIUM / HARD	34.75	-13.4	515
08	WOODCOTE SOUTH	MEDIUM / HARD	27	-	440
09	NETTLEBED	EASY / HARD	27.9 OR 10.7	+10.7 & +10	420
10	WATLINGTON	MEDIUM / HARD	39	-12.9 or +3	770
11	IBSTONE	MEDIUM / HARD	31.7	+7.6 & +3.8	800
12	CHINNOR	MEDIUM	32.1	+1.6 & +3 or -7.4	630
13	PRINCESS RISBOROUGH	EASY & MEDIUM	10.2 OR 35.8	-	785
14	TRING	MEDIUM	31.6	-5.6	460
15	WOBURN	EASY / HARD	VARIOUS	-	-
16	GREAT OFFLEY	EASY / MEDIUM	29.8	-14 & -2.25 or +7.9	380
17	LETTY GREEN	EASY	33	-20 & -10 or +4	425
18	CHICKSANDS	EASY / EXTREME	37.2	Various	260

ROUTE INFORMATION

Mostly double track, which gets more technical the faster you go, making it suitable for all abilities. Gets slippery when wet, and the 4x4's can churn up the trail, where it hasn't been resurfaced.

This route is very similar to the northern route, but a bit harder. There are shortcut options though, and navigation is easy, so the going is quick. Do both rides together for 1 hard loop. Slippery when wet.

This route is pretty easy to navigate as it uses a long section of the Ridgeway, which provides a goo dlong stretch of double track that is mostly made up of a good surface, along the ridge top, so also drains quite well. The route uses a variety of trails, and has shortcut and extension options, so it should be suitable for all riders. Although it drains well it is best avoided when wet, as 4x4's can damage it.

The outward leg (along the Ridgeway) is easy to navigate, and you will cover the ground quickly, but is exposed and can get damaged by 4x4's in the wet. The next section uses some quieter tracks and country roads, and their is plenty of opportunity to extend the ride, before a fun descent back to the start.

The rutted doubletrack of the Ridgeway basically provides a choice of single track trails, some of which work out well, others into deep pedal catching ruts - its all part of the fun as you race your mates. The 2nd part of the ride uses nice quiet bridleways and country lanes, before a steep downhill to finish.

The main route is more of a guide to get you to some areas where there is lots more on offer with a bit of exploring. There is lots of single track to find, but navigation is tricky. Go when its dry.

A great route, using some superb single track trails, and a few opportunities to change the distance. Very fit riders could join the 2 routes together to make 1 'Killer' ride. Muddy, but rideable in the wet.

This route has some great bits of single track, including a great section alongside the river (just be careful of walkers and steps at the start). Hard going and slippery in the wet.

A lovely ride with a shortcut and extension to provide a combination of routes, making it suitable for all. Most of the trails cope well in the wet (unlike a lot of the trails in this area) so it can be a good place to head in the winter - just don't expect to stay dry and mud-free.

A long hard ride, but with plenty of shortcut opportunities and plenty of fast single track, that gets more technical the faster you go - so its good for all abilities. Its best tackled in the dry as the fun is in the speed, which is lost when the trails get wet and soft - the tree roots are also very slippery in the wet.

With 7 hills, you are nearly always going either up or down, and their is plenty of single track, which all takes it toll. However there are plenty of shortcut options, and some great country pubs to have a pint and a breather at. Some low lying tracks suffer in the wet, and its tough anyway, so do it when dry.

This ride starts with a steep technical descent, but otherwise its pretty suitable for most riders. There are a variety of great tracks on this route, but it does suffer in wet weather.

There are a few steep hills and some tricky sections of rooty single track, so the main route may not be suitable for novices, but the short (easy) ride will be. Any wet weather will make the roots extra slippery, but otherwise it isn't too bad. Also, check out Aston Hill MTB area by Wendover Woods.

There are some short steep climbs, and some nice single track, which should be suitable for all abilities. The trails are generally ok in the as the area is not over used, but the going will be harder.

There are lots of unmarked trails throughout the woods here. To get the best from it you need a local to follow, but if like exploring by yourself, you will undoubtedly find some great trails and not get too lost, as it isn't the biggest of areas.

Easy navigation on well draining tracks, and not too technical, make this a good wet ride. The extension and shortcut options also means it makes a good ride for all abilities. There is also a nice section of single track along Oughton river.

This is quite an easy going ride, with enough shortcuts to make it suitable for most riders. It also copes pretty well in bad weather, so it makes a good wet weather ride when all others are falling apart.

By car, just head for Rowney Warren Wood, as there areenough trails there to keep you entertained. If arriving by train, follow our off-road route to the woods, where you will find 2 XC courses, a duel slalom, downhills and jumps. Something for everyone, and it fairs ok in the wet weather too.

mountain bike rides

in and around

the

chilterns

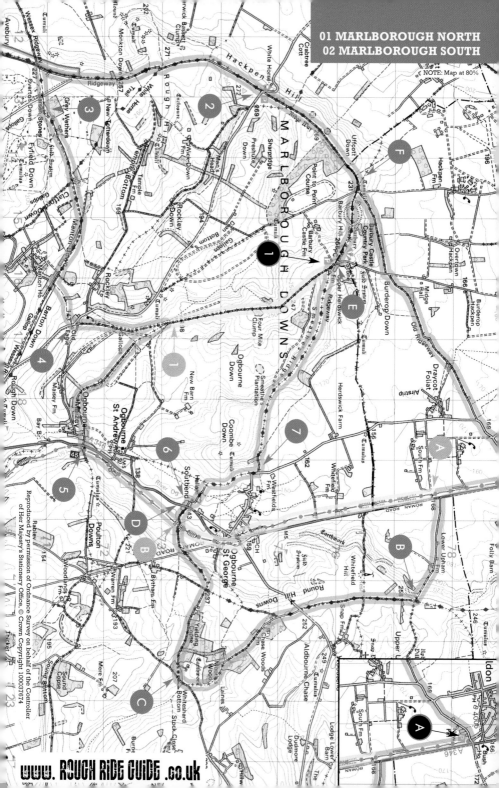

www.ROUGH RiDE GUIDE .co.uk

NORTH ROUTE

25KM (15.5) 400 metres of climbing

1 START. Go west, to/through Barbury Castle, on a BW, DH to a rd and turn R, then immediately L on the Ridgeway (SU 145/764). 2.4km (1.5m) to a rd (129/747), and go SA into car park (White Horse on the hillside here).

2 Go along the Ridgeway for 4.2km (2.6m) at a X-tracks and a board welcoming you to Fyfield Down Nature Reserve (125/709) turn L over a gate into the Nature Reserve. Head over grassy BW for 0.5km (0.3m) then across the Gallops on to a gravel track.

3 UH on this track to a gate, and keep SA, DH to the valley bottom and go R. After 1.1km (0.7m) go L on a BW (161/ 711), 0.15km past a DT BW on the L, DH to a rd (168/714) and go L on it, then bear R on a track.

4 Immediately crossing a rd, keep SA on a good track for 1.45km (0.9m) to a X-tracks (168/730). Turn R, UH, on a ByW or see shortcut. Past the gallops, DH, to corner of a rd in Ogbourne Maizey and keep SA/L to A346 (188/716)

5 Cross this rd to the cycletrack on the other side, by a metal bridge, and turn L on this cycletrack (old railway). Follow this for 2.1km (1.3m) to where the Ridgeway crosses you (201/733) and go L on this, DH to the A346 rd.

6 Go SA on the rd opposite, UH, past the houses to a T-J (194/738), and turn R (north) and follow this to a rd. Go SA/L on the rd, then shortly turn L (west) off it, back off-road on the Ridgeway (192/747).

7 Follow the Ridgeway, UH, for 4km (2.5m) to a T-J (158 /759) at the top and turn R. Just up here turn L through a single gate (opposite the farm, and before the Frog & Spoon cafe) on a BW, back to the car park (157/761).

SHORTCUT:

-7.25KM (4.5M) -140 metres climbing

1 Keep SA on this good track, UH, for another 3.2km (2m) (becoming tarmac at the end, and Ridgeway joins from the R), past the Frog and Spoon cafe on the R and turn L through a gate back to the car park (157/761).

SOUTH ROUTE

24.1KM (15M) 380 metres of climbing

A START. Go south on 'Chiseldon to Marlborough' cycle path, for 1.6km (1m), then go L to the A346 rd (SU 196/ 777) or see shortcut. Turn L on this rd, then shortly R to Lower Upham farm. Go past the farm, on a stony track, UH, to a X-tracks with Ridgeway at top (213/774).

B Turn R (south) on the Ridgeway, for 2km (1.25m) to a rd (215/ 754) and go SA on the drive. Continue on this past the farm (or stay on the Ridgeway to -2.4km/1.5m), DH, bearing R, to a DT at the bottom, turn R, then shortly R again at a fork (227/733)

C Follow this UH, to the top and keep SA, then just before you start descending bear L following the Ridgeway signposts, DH. To a minor rd and keep SA, and follow this down to the main rd (198/734) or see shortcut.

D Go SA on the Ridgeway, UH, to a T-J (194/738) and turn R (north) and follow this to a rd and go SA/L on the rd. Shortly turn L (west) back off-road, on the Ridgeway and follow this DT, UH for about 4km (2.5m) to a T-J (158/759) at the top and turn R.

E Shortly turn L through a single gate (opposite the farm, and before the cafe) on a BW, past a car park (157/ 761). Through a gate on a grassy track through Barbury Castle, DH to a rd. Turn R, then R again on a ByW (Old Ridgeway Chiseldon).

F DH, 1.45km (0.9m) to a rd and turn L then R (effectively SA) back onto the ByW (159/769). Follow this rough track, and keep SA as it becomes tarmac, joining a rd and keep SA/L. 0.4km (0.25m) to a X-rds and go SA then just past New Farm go R, back to the car park (193/793).

SHORTCUT:

2 options

Use the cycle path between Ogbourne St George and Chiseldon on either the outward or return leg of the route:

A -5.2km/3.2m & 160 metres of climbing

B -6.6km/4.1m & 155 metres of climbing

GETTING THERE: Train station in Swindon, follow the Sustrans cycle route no.45 from the station, for 13km/8m to Chiseldon.

East route starts from a car park by Chiseldon - exit the M4 at junction 15, go south on the A346 for 1 mile, then turn R at a X-roads (just past the petrol station), and the car park (height restriction) is on the left (192/793).

West route starts at Barbury Castle - follow the B4005 through Chiseldon and turn L on a RHB, to Barbur Castle car park (157/761).

BIKE SHOPS: There is plenty of choice in Swindon e.g. Mitchell Cycles on 01793 523306, Swindon Cycles on 01793 700105 and Red Planet Bikes on 01793 522211.

ACCOMMODATION: B&B at Manor Farm in Avebury on 01672 539294 B&B at Browns Farm in Marlborough on 01672 515129 Crockford@Farming.co.uk) Marlborough TI on 01672 513989 Wiltshire Cycling hotline (with accommodation info) on 01980 623255

REFRESHMENTS: East route: Pub in Chiseldon and a cafe at the Esso garage, and a cafe by Barbury Castle. West route: cafe at Barbury castle and a pub in Ogbourne St Andrew.

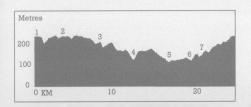

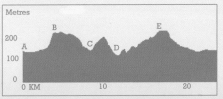

29.5KM (18.4M) 480 metres of climbing

❶ START. Go back to the main (Court Hill) rd and turn L (north) for 0.3km (0.2m) (over water) and keep SA/L on Windmill hill rd (East Challow). After 0.3km (0.2m) UH on this rd, turn L on a ByW (SU 380/873), for 2.25km (1.4m) to a rd going 3-ways, and go on the B4001 rd, UH for 2km (1.25m) then L on the Ridgeway (rd on R) (344/851).

Quick directions: Keep SA on the Ridgeway (RW) for 11.1km (6.9m), and the rejoin directions at no.5.

❷ Keep SA on the Ridgeway for 5.6km (3.5m) to the A338 rd (394/844).

❸ Go R on the rd them immediately L back on the RW, for 1.2km (0.75m) and turn R at a T-J (then keep L on the Ridgeway), for 0.55km (0.35m) to a fork (410/841), and bear L (staying on Ridgeway) or see **extension 1**.

❹ Go to and over the B4494 rd (418/841) and SA on the Ridgeway for another 3km (1.9m) or see the shortcut.

❺ Shortly after some trees on the L, and a DT crossing the RW, turn L, DH, on ST BW (445/851) or see **extension 2**. **5a** - DH for 1.45km (0.9m) to a rd, and go R on this, into East Ginge (448/866), staying sharp L on the rd, for 1km (0.6m) turn L on the ByW which crosses the rd (446/875).

❻ After 1.45km (0.9m) join a rd and keep SA/L, then very shortly turn L on a DT, bearing sharp R (432/875). 0.5km (0.3m) to a rd (429/870) and turn R/SA on this, for 0.6m past a church, and turn L on a rd (West Lockinge), just post a car park & telephone box (425/876).

❼ After 0.25km (0.15m) turn L through a farm (421/877), and follow this BW for 2.6km (1.6m) then turn R on a DT (417/853) by the hedges, after a small climb and before the slight DH, to the B4494 rd (413/853).

❽ Go SA on the ByW for 1.8km (1.1m) to a A338 rd (396/852) and go L on rd, steep UH for 0.4km (0.25m). Turn R on Court hill rd (394/849), DH for 2.2km (1.35m) then turn L, back in to Letcombe Regis/the end (382/866).

EXTENSION 1

+5KM (3.1M) +65 metres of climbing

❶ Bear R at the fork (off the RW), 1.4km (0.85m) to a rd (420/833), cross this, through a gate. Through the middle of a field, (farm on L), for 1.6km (1m) to a rd (430/821).

❷ Turn L on the rd for 0.8km (0.5m) (through Farnborough) then R on a BW just past a red phone box (437/820). 1.2km (0.75m) to X-tracks in the woods (449/816), turn L, which bears L, out of woods.

❸ SA for 1.6km (1m), DH to a rd (448/833), and go SA (RHS of the house) on a BW, through a farm. 1.95km (1.2m) to a X-tracks with the RW (443/850) and turn R for 0.25km (0.15m) then L on a ST, and rejoin the route at no.5a or see **extension 2**

SHORTCUT

-10.5KM (6.5M) -140 metres of climbing

❶ Turn L on a BW (off the RW) immediately after crossing the rd, DH, keeping SA at the X-rds after 0.55km (0.35m). After another 0.8km (0.5m) turn L on a DT, (417/853), by the hedges, and turn L to the B4494 rd, and rejoin the main route at no.8.

EXTENSION 2

+4.5KM (2.8M) +70 metres of climbing

Ⓐ Keep SA on the Ridgeway for another 1.8km (1.1m), (0.5km/0.3m past a rough car park) and turn L on a rough DT BW (462/849) (don't worry the track improves). DH for 0.7km (0.45m) to a X-tracks and keep SA alongside the high (research laboratories) fence on the R, for 1.3km (0.8m) to a fork (466/867).

Ⓑ Bear R at the fork (by the old tyres & tank), for 0.8km (0.5m) then bear L on the BW, into the trees (473/871). After 0.65km (0.4m) at a X-tracks (475/877), turn L on the DT ByW.

Ⓒ Keep SA on this ByW for 2.8km (1.75m) to the 2and rd crossing (446/875) and rejoin the main route at no.6.

GETTING THERE: The ride starts from Letcombe Regis, which is just south west of Wantage (where the A 338 and A417 cross). Aim for Wantage then head west on the B4507 (Ickleton rd) signposted 'Ashbury'. After 1 mile turn left to Letcombe Regis, on Court hill rd, then right on main street into the village (382/866) and park considerately. Train station in Didcot, about 8km/5m away - go through Harwell on the B449, then right on the A417 and join the route at extension 2, letter C.

ACCOMMODATION: B&B's in Letcombe Regis on: 01235 762860 and 765827. Note; the YHA just south of Wantage is now closed. For more options call Wantage T.I. on: 01235 760176.

BIKE SHOP: Ridgeway Cycles in Wantage on 01235 764445.

REFRESHMENTS: There is a pub in Letcombe Regis and a choice of places in Wantage, and a pub just off the main route in Ardington.

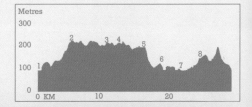

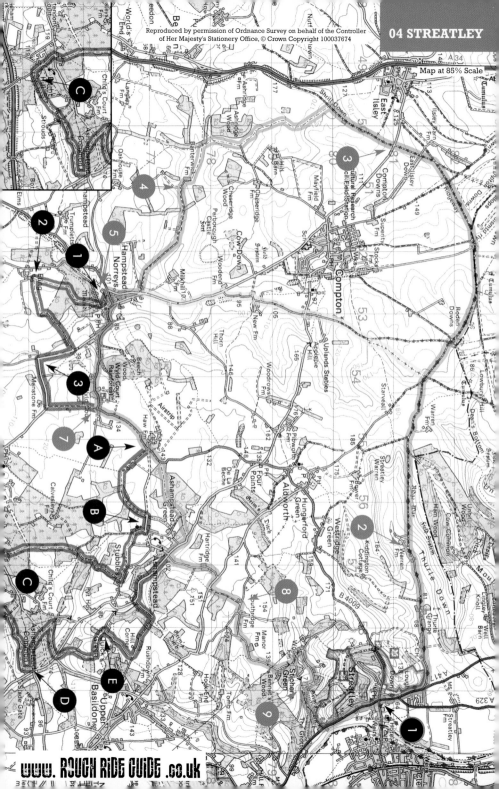

Map at 85% Scale

29KM (18M) 495 metres of climbing

1 **START**. From the X-rds (in Streatley, by the pub) head north (pub behind you) on the A329, for 0.3km (0.2m) then bear L on the A417 (Wantage). After 0.4km (0.25m) turn L on Rectory rd (Ridgeway) (SU 589/814), and follow this for 2.25km (1.4m) to Warren farm.

2 Keep SA/R, UH on the Ridgeway, and stay on the Ridgeway (main DT) for 6.5km (4m) or see the shortcut. At some X-tacks (508/819) (1.1km/0.7m after a bridge that goes over nothing), go SA (East Ilsley) as the Ridgeway goes R. After 0.3km (0.2m) at another X-tracks (506/817) turn L, DH to a rd (503/810).

3 Go SA on the BW for 1.3km (0.8m), UH, to a blue height limit sign and turn L on a (grassy) rough and rutty BW (497/799), (you can probably hear the A34 rd, SA). After 1.1m bear R at a fork, for another 0.65km (0.4m) to a X-tracks (in some woods) (503/778).

4 Turn L, into a field, becoming a DT by a farm and keep SA on this for 2.1km (1.3m) to a rd and turn sharp R, to a T-J (526/763).

5 Turn L over a bridge, on the B4009 through the village, or see extension 1. As you exit the village, keep L at the fork on the B4009 (Wyld court rainforest) for 2.4km (1.5m) to a rd on the R (559/761). Stay on the B4009 or see extension 2, 0.25km (0.15m) then turn R on a BW into the woods (553/771).

6 Keep SA for 1.4km (0.85m), DH to a rd (565/776) and turn R on this for 0.4km (0.25m) to a X-rds (568/772) and L on Hartridge lane. **6A** - R at a T-J after 1km (0.6m) (Upper Basildon) for 0.15km (0.1m) then L on a BW at Blackwood house (574/780), SA to a rd (576/784).

7 Turn R on the rd, and keep L on this for 1m then bear L on a ByW as the rd goes DH and R, DH to a rd (583/795). Turn R on this, to a T-J (589/794) and turn L, UH on a drive (Ash Hill), between the brick posts.

8 After 0.3km (0.2m) go SA on a BW, as the drive bears L, steep DH on a ST to the A417 rd (595/798). Turn L on this for 1.6km (1m) back to the X-rds/lights in Streatley (591/808) (pub on L), and the end of the ride.

SHORTCUT:
-6km (3.7M) -120 metres of climbing

1 After 2.9km (1.8m) (from Warren farm) turn L at a X-tracks (540/815) on a ByW (just after a ByW joins from the L). DH for 2.2km (1.35m), joining Downs road, and keep SA to a X-rds (530/795) and go SA on Coombe rd for 1km (0.6m) to New farm (527/787).

2 Go past the farm to a fork and bear L, to another rd and bear L on this. After 1.4km (0.85m) bear R at a fork (526/768), to a T-J and rejoin the main route at no.5.

EXTENSION 1:
+3.2KM (2M) +50 metres of climbing

1 Just over the bridge turn R towards the village hall, and into some woods and turn R on a BW as soon as you enter these woods (528/761). Keep SA to a fence (525/755) and turn R, across a field to the other side (524/751).

2 Turn L in front of the house (unmarked BW), along field edge for 0.55km (0.35) to the far end and turn L. Through some woods and over a stream, then UH to a rd (535/757) and turn R on this for 0.5km (0.3m) then turn L on another rd (Yattendon 1m) (537/751).

3 After 0.7km (0.45m) go L on a BW (opposite Manstone farm) (545/753) as rd bears R. Keep SA as this becomes a concrete track, to the B4009 rd (545/761) and turn R/SA on the rd. After 1.1km (0.7m) stay on the B4009 or see extension 2, for 0.25km (0.15m) then go R on a BW into the wood (553/771) and rejoin main route at no.6.

EXTENSION 2:
+10.5KM (6.5M) 160 metres climbing

A Turn R on the BW before the rd on the R (opposite the white house), through a green gate and turn L on a concrete track, bearing L (555/765) to a rd. Turn R on this for 0.25km (0.15m) then turn R on Church lane) as you enter the village (564/769).

B Turn L just past the church on a R.O.W. (565/767), through a field, bearing R parallel with a rd. To a thatched cottage (572/765) and turn R on the DT BW, and keep SA for 2km (1.25m) to a rd and go SA on a ST rd, for 0.4km (0.25m) then L after HGV sign (570/743) on a BW.

C Keep SA for 1km (0.6m) (SA at X-tracks and SA/L by a house), to a X-tracks (ByW on R & ROW on L) (578/746). Go SA then immediately bear R at the fork and ride along the bottom (RHS) of the wood for 1.1km (0.7m), bearing L to a T-J (586/750), near a rd, and turn L.

D 0.3km (0.2m) to a fork and turn R , UH to a rd and go SA/R, to the edge of the wood (579/753) and turn R. After 0.55km (0.35m) at a rd (584/754), turn L on the BW, UH to a T-J and bear L, to a rd by some houses (580/762).

E Turn R on the rd for 0.65km (0.4m) then go L on a BW as the rd bears sharp R (584/767). Keep to the R of converted barns, and bearing L, DH to a rd (575/767). Turn R on this rd for 1.1km (0.7m) to a X-rds (568/773) and turn R on Hartridge lane, and rejoin main route at no.6a.

GETTING THERE: The ride starts in Streatley, where the A417, A329, B4009 and B4526 meet, by the river Thames. There are places to park off the A417 on the road to Thurle Down (GR 587/815). There is also a free car park in Goring, just over the river (follow the signs). There is also a train station in Goring.

BIKE SHOPS: Trail Junkies nr Moulsford (GR 585/829), tel: 01491 871721, and Mountain High in Pangbourne on: 0118 984 1851.

REFRESHMENTS: Pubs in Streatley and Goring, and a shop in Goring. The only pub on the route is the White Heart in Hampstead Norreys

ACCOMMODATION: B&B in Goring on: 01491 872829, and in 01491 Streatley on: 872048. YHA in Streatley on: 0870 770 6054, Camping in Wallingford on: 01491 836860, and Wallingford T.I. on: 01491 826972.

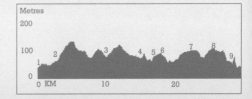

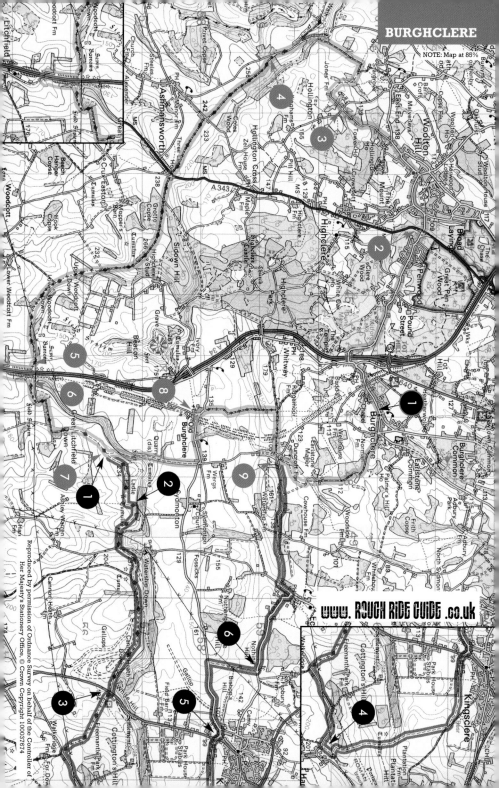

NOTE: Map at 85%

www.ROUGH RIDE GUIDE.co.uk

Reproduced by permission of Ordnance Survey on behalf of the Controller of Her Majesty's Stationery Office. © Crown Copyright 100037674

27.4 (17M) 490 metres of climbing

1 START. Go back to the main (Harts) rd and go L on it for 1.1km (0.7m), through Burghclere, bearing L, and take 2and R (bridge over the A34 rd). Follow this rd for 2.7km (1.7m) to a X-rds (with A343) and go SA (Highclere).

2 0.25km (0.15m) to a T-J (SU 436/618) and turn L on this rd for 0.8km (0.5m), then turn L on Church Rd (by the church) (430/617). 0.7km (0.45m) to a fork in the rd, and bear L (Hollington), 1km (0.65m) to a grass triangle and bear R, then SA/L on a BW (rd) (419/603).

3 Becomes off-road, and bears R to the corner of a track (413/606) and turn L on this. Keep L, UH to a rd (407/599) and turn L on this for 0.8km (0.5m), then bear L on the Wayfarers Walk (WW), ByW (410/592).

Quick guide: Stay on 'Wayfarers walk' for 7.6km (4.7m) to the A34 rd (463/551) and rejoin the route at no.5.

4 2.8km (1.75m) to the A343 rd (430/575), bear L then R back on the WW. After 2.25km (1.4m) (going DH), bear R after the metal gates as the DT bears L, to the top of the field. Through a field to some metal gates and bear L, into the woods, to the A34 rd (462/551).

5 Turn R just before the rd, which bears L under the bridge (A34) and immediately turn L into a field (not sign-posted) (462/545). Follow the LHS of the field (parallel to the rd) for 0.8km (0.5m) (old bridge on the L), then turn R, up the valley (463/551).

6 After 1.2km (0.75m), turn L on another DT, following the white wooden arrow (472/555), near some woods. After 1.1km (0.7m) on this, bear L at a very feint fork (476/564), before the top of the hill, or see the extension.

7 DH, to the LHS of the hill top, going north, along the BW track for 1.6km (1m) to a rd (477/579). Turn L, into Old Burghclere, over a bridge, bearing R, then keep SA on the ByW, as the rd bears L, (468/580).

8 1.2km (0.75m) to a X-tracks (469/593) and turn R, for 0.8km (0.5m), to a rd and turn L, then immediately bear R at the rd fork, then turn immediately L on a BW (477/593), before another rd T-J.

9 0.7km (0.45m) to a DT and turn L on this, then shortly R on the BW (if this is overgrown - follow the DT, past the manor, and rejoin the BW. Follow this to a X-rds at a grass triangle, (472/610) and go SA (Church lane) back to the car (470/610).

EXTENSION:

+17.2KM (10.7M) +320 metres climbing

1 Bear R at the fork (staying on the WW), then shortly, keep SA through the gates, as track bears R. To the top of the hill and bear R on grassy a DT, to a T-J and turn (sharp) L for 0.15km then turn R through the wooden gate, by a green gate (484/568).

2 Through the field, and bear L at a metal gate, onto a good track (under the elec. cables), UH to a rd (491/566). Go SA on a ST BW, UH through some wooden gates, and join a DT, bearing L and follow this for 1.95km (1.2m), to a rd (515/564).

3 Turn L on the rd, then immediately (sharp) R on the (WW) BW and follow this for 1.3km (0.8m) to a rd (525/556). Turn L on the rd (leaving the WW) for 0.9m, then turn L on a BW through some metal gates (538/558), just before entering Hannington village.

4 Bear sharp L at end of the field, and keep SA/L for 2km (1.25m) to a T-J (535/580) at the end of a path through the middle of a field Turn L, to a fork and bear L on the ST, and keep SA, becoming a drive, to a rd.

5 Turn R on the rd, then immediately L on Bear Hill rd (by some houses), over the stream, to a T-J (522/583). Turn L on this rd (Sydmonton) for 1.2km (0.75m), then turn R on a BW (large stone in the middle) (510/581), for 0.8km (0.5m) to a rd (512/589).

6 Turn L on the rd for 1.5km (0.95m) to a T-J in Ecchinswell village, (Royal Oak pub here), and turn L, for 0.25km (0.15m) then turn R on another rd (497/593) (Burchclere). After 2.25km (1.4m) bear R at the fork (477/593), and immediately turn R again on a BW (before the blue HGV sign) and rejoin the main route at no.9.

GETTING THERE: Start in Burghclere, just off the A34, south of Newbury. Follow the signs for Burghclere off the A34 and go through the village, past the Carpenters Arms pub, then turn R on Church lane (by the church) and park in the lay-by on the left just here (470/610). Train station in Newbury - go south on A339 then SA/south at a roundabout, to Burghclere.

ACCOMMODATION: B&B in Burchclere on: 01635 278305, B&B in Newtown on: 01635 43097, Camping at Oakley farm (off the A343), on: 01635 36581. Newbury T.I. on: 01635 30267

BIKE SHOP: Cycle Shop in Newbury on: 01635 582100

REFRESHMENTS: Pub in Burghclere, just off the route in Woolton hill and Ashmansworth. More in Hannington, Kingsclere & Ecchinswell on the extension.

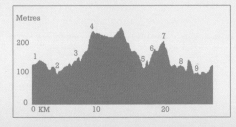

NOTE: Map at 90%

18.5KM (11.5M) 140 metres of climbing

❶ START. Go back to the fork in the rough DT (entrance to the car park), and turn L. After 0.15km (0.1m) keep SA on a ST, leaving the DT as it bears L (by a house) and go SA. To a better track, at the edge of the trees (SU 821/594) and turn R on this, to a rd. Go SA on the BW, for 0.3km (0.2m) to an old (disused) tarmac rd (816/593), and bear R on this, to a rd (814/594) (Dungells rd on the R).

❷ Turn L over the main (Vigo) rd, onto an off-road ST (no sign), and keep SA on this to an old runway. Keep SA on the runway (or the ST to the RHS), bearing R, to some houses at the end (806/598), and turn L on a better (newer) runway. After 0.5km (0.3m) turn R off the runway, as it bears L (before some old, large metal gates) to face the airport, on a ST, into the trees (802/596).

❸ To a T-J, by a fence, and turn L, alongside the fence, for 0.5km (0.3m) to a (dirty) sign and turn R on the stony (permissive BW) track. Follow this around the quarry, then R on the BW into the woods. Emerge by a barrier, by a rd (788/595) and bear R/SA on a permissive path, parallel to the rd on your RHS or see the extension.

❹ Exit by quarry entrance and go SA/L on the rd to A327 (786/591). Go L on this for 0.65km (0.4m) to the A30 and go SA (L then R) on Black-bushes rd. Turn L after 0.5km (0.3m) into Yateley Heath wood (opposite Ivyhill Hole rd). After 0.8km (0.5m) on main DT turn R on the (3rd) track (797/582).

❺ Keep SA on this forest track for 1.3km (0.8m) to a rd (801/571) and go L on this for 1.2km (0.75m) to a T-J (B3013) (811/567). Go SA, over the rd, past an old arch gate house on the L, onto a BW. Keep SA (R then L) over a DT after 0.8km (0.5m) for 0.5km (0.3m), past a pylon, and turn L then shortly R (east) on a DT (no signs), to the A327 rd.

❻ Cross the rd into the woods, and keep SA on the BW for 0.15m to some X-tracks (834/573) with a grassy DT SA. Turn R on a BW, to a for and bear L,

for 0.3km (0.2m) then turn L on the (DT) BW (837/572) (lake on your LHS). Just before you exit the trees to the sandy lake side, turn R over a small (hidden) wooden bridge, into the woods.

❼ Follow this ST, keeping L, to the south-east edge of the lake. Turn L over a small bridge, then immediately turn R on a BW, to a (BW) T-J (843/574) and turn L, for 0.4km (0.25m) to a (BW) X-tracks (846/576). Turn L on the wide BW track, which joins a tarmac rd, then leaves it at a T-J (after 0.65km/0.4m), keep SA (off-road) on the BW.

❽ 0.3km (0.2m) to a multiple X-tracks and turn L then immediately R (effectively SA), UH. 0.4km (0.25m) to an off-set X-tracks, and go SA (L then R) to a T-J (840/587) and turn R. After 0.25km (0.15m) turn L on a DT, following the telegraph poles, DH, and keep SA to the duel carriageway at the bottom (840/593).

• **NOTE**: There are lots of (good) tracks in Yateley Common, so we recommend you explore it and make your own way back from here - or see no.9.

❾ Cross the rd (carefully) and go SA on the BW opposite, and shortly turn L on the first ST you see. Parallel to the A30 rd on the LHS for 2km (1.25m) then go R (north) for 0.65km (0.4m) to some houses and a track back to the car park (821/596).

EXTENSION:

Various

❶ Keep SA and follow the BW (DT) through Warren Heath, to Bramshill Plantation (there are some nice trails in here, but we are not aware of the legal status for riding in here). Turn around and head back to the route.

• **NOTE**: It is also well worth exploring Yateley Common and Eversely Common further, as there are lots of fun trails to be ridden.

GETTING THERE: Exit the M4 at junction 4a and go north on the A327 to a roundabout with the A30 and go straight ahead (Cricket hill lane) for 1/2 mile then turn right (by a telephone box) on a rough track bearing left at the fork, into the (free) Yateley common car park (821/596). Railway station in Blackwater or Fleet, both just off the route.

ACCOMMODATION: B&B's in Fleet on: 01252 816924 and 623755. Camping in Finchampstead on: 0118 9733928. No YHA's close by. Fleet T.I. on: 01252 811151.

BIKE SHOP: Cycle Kingdom in Fleet: 01252 624136.

REFRESHMENTS: A pub near the start / end of the ride or shops, pubs, take-aways in Yateley.

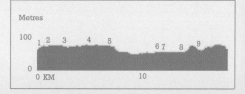

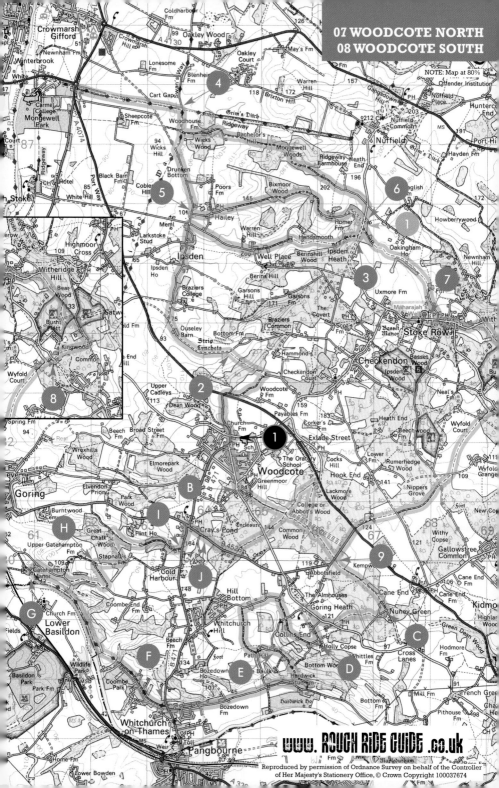

NOTE: Map at 80%

www.ROUGH RIDE GUIDE.co.uk

Reproduced by permission of Ordnance Survey on behalf of the Controller of Her Majesty's Stationery Office, © Crown Copyright 100037674

NORTH ROUTE

34.75KM (21.6M) 515 metres climbing

❶ START. Exit the car park and turn L on the rd to some X-rds and turn R for 0.8km (0.5m) to the A4074 rd (SU 643/827). Cross the rd onto the track opposite and keep L on this for 1km (0.6m) then turn L on a BW, as the rd bears R (650/831), DH, through the woods, to a rd. Good private (RATZ club) XC course in here.

❷ Turn L on the rd for 1.3km (0.8m) to a fork (633/840) and bear R (Ipsden), keeping SA for 1.6km (1m) to a X-rds (638/857). Turn R on the rd for 1.3km (0.8m), then keep SA on a BW, as the rd bears R (647/852) and follow this for 1.95km (1.2m), UH, to a rd (667/854) and turn L for 0.5km (0.3m) to a X-rds (668/859) or see the shortcut.

❸ Turn L (dead end) on the BW and keep SA, DH, on this for 3km (1.9m) to a fork by some woods and bear R on a DT, past a farm, to a rd (636/872). Turn R on rd for 0.3km (0.2m) then L on the Ridgeway BW (636/875).

❹ SA over a minor rd after 0.65km (0.4m), for 1.45km (0.9m) to a gate (617/ 879) by the A4074 rd. Turn around and go back the way you came to the 2and rd (636/875) and go R on this for 0.65km (0.4m). L at the rd T-J for 1.1km (0.7m) then L on the rd (637/858) (Hailey).

❺ Past the King William pub, becoming a rough DT, UH, for 3.55km (2.2m) to a rd and turn R then shortly L on a BW (668/856) and follow this BW.

❻ After 1.6km (1m) join a drive and keep SA on this for another 0.55km (0.35m) to a T-J (681/841). Turn L on the rd (or R to a shop) for 0.9km (0.55m), past a pub, then turn R on a BW opposite Clare house (689/840), UH.

❼ 0.7km (0.45m) to a fork and bear R past wooden posts, to a fork and bear R, over a DT, to a T-J (694/831). Turn L to a rd and turn R on this for 0.5km (0.3) then R on a BW (697/828). Keep SA through the woods, to a drive and go SA on a BW, to L of Holly Tree cottage (693/827).

❽ DH, to a rd and keep SA on the (Hazel grove) BW (pub on left), keeping to the LHS of some houses, for 3.6km (2.25m), over a drive and 3 minor rds) to the A4074 rd. Go SA on the rd opposite (Goring) for 0.65km (0.4m) then turn R on a BW (663/800).

❾ SA for 1.95km (1.2m) out of the woods, onto a drive and keep SA/L on this for 0.25km (0.15m) to a rd (645/812). Turn R on this, to a fork and bear L, DH, 0.65km (0.4m) to a T-J by a shop and turn R. 0.15km (0.1m) to X-rds and turn R back to the car park on the R (645/820).

SHORTCUT:

-13.4KM (8.3M) -210 metres climbing

❶ Shortly turn R off the rd, on a BW (681/841), and rejoin the main route at no.6.

SOUTH ROUTE

27KM (16.8M) 440 metres of climbing

❶ START. Exit the car park and turn L on the rd to some X-rds, and turn L (past an pub), for 0.15km (0.1m) then L on Whitehouse rd (by the Post Office). UH, 0.65km (0.4m) to a T-J (645/814) and turn R for 0.15km (0.1m) then L on a BW (Green Lane) opposite a rd on the R (646/812).

Ⓑ After 0.25km (0.15m) keep SA/R into the woods, as the drive bears L, 0.8km (0.5m) to a X-tracks (654/808). Turn L to the A4074 (659/814), then R and follow the white arrows. To a DT and turn L, to a rd. Go SA on the BW for 1.3km (0.8m) (keep L at the stagnant water, becoming a DT, to a fork by a house (672/791) and go R.

Ⓒ After 0.25km (0.15m) turn R on a BW, bearing L around the stagnant water, to a rd (663/789) and turn R on this. 0.65km (0.4m) to some X-rds (658/792) by the old post office and turn L immediately L again on a BW, by the red phone box. 0.55km (0.35m) to a X-rds and turn R to a fork (658/786) and bear R on a BW.

Ⓓ Go over a rd after 0.65km (0.4m), for 0.3km (0.2m) to another rd (653/794) and go L on this for 0.7km (0.45m) then and turn L on a BW (646/792). UH, along, then DH to a rd (649/784) and turn L on this, steep UH, for 0.4km (0.25m) then R on a drive, as the rd bears L (652/785).

Ⓔ Keep SA on the DT, into the woods, follow this main track, R then L, DH, to a drive (658/778). Turn R on this for 0.7km (0.45m), past some stables, to a X-rds and keep SA on the rd (although shortly after the farm, there is a ST in the trees on the R, parallel to the rd) for 1.8km (1.1m) to a T-J (634/775) in Whitchurch.

Ⓕ Turn R, UH, for 100 metres then go L on the Thames path BW (by a 40mph sign) for 1.2km (0.75m) and keep SA. Keep SA on this ST for 2.4km (1.5m) to a X-tracks (610/798) by some houses, and turn R on the stony DT.

Ⓖ UH, to a rd and turn R on this for 0.5km (0.3m) then keep SA, on the ROW as the rd bears L. UH, for 0.8km (0.5m) to a fork (623/795) and bear L to/on the rd (this is a FP). Turn R after 0.5km (0.3m) on a BW (old hut on L), on a thin ST, on the RHS of the fence.

Ⓗ Into the woods and keep SA for 0.65km (0.4m) to a fork (625/799) and turn L, DH, keep R at fork after 0.4km (0.25m), to a T-J at the bottom in the open (624/805). Turn R and keep SA for 1.4km (0.85m) UH, through gates, past a house, join a drive, to a rd (636/801).

Ⓘ Turn L on the rd for 0.4km (0.25m) to an (off-set) X-rds (637/806) (pub SA) and go R on the B4526 rd (Reading). After 1km (0.6m) turn L on easy to miss (Exlade) BW (645/801) and keep SA on this ST for 0.65km (0.4m) to a rd.

Ⓙ Go SA on the BW for 0.5km (0.3m) to a X-tracks (654/808) been here before. Turn L and retrace your tracks back to the start (UH to rd, go R, L at fork, to T-J by the shop, go R, to X-rds, turn R to the car park) (645/820).

GETTING THERE: Start from the free car park in Woodcote, by the village hall (645/820). Woodcote is north-west of Reading, just off the A4074. Train stations in Goring and Pangbourne off south route.

ACCOMMODATION: Wallingford T.I. on: 01491826972

BIKE SHOPS: Mountain High in Pangbourne: 01189 841851 & Rides on Air in Wallingford: 01491 836289

REFRESHMENTS: Shop and pubs in Woodcote. North route: pubs in Hailey, Stoke Row. South route; pubs in Goring Heath, Whitchurch and Crays pond.

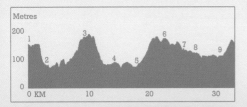

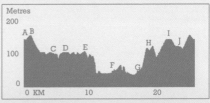

09 NETTLEBED

Map at 90% Scale

www.ROUGH RIDE GUIDE.co.uk

Reproduced by permission of Ordnance Survey on behalf of the Controller
of Her Majesty's Stationery Office, © Crown Copyright 100037674

27.9KM (17.3M) 420 metres climbing

❶ START (SU 702/868). Head east on Old Kiln road in Nettlebed, away from the main rd, and take the 1st L or see the short ride. Take 1st L on a rough track, for 0.65km (0.4m) to a rd (709/ 864) in Catslip and turn R (south) to main rd and go SA on a BW. Follow the white arrows, DH on ST, to a DT (707/858), FP SA, and turn L on the DT.

❷ To a DT (709/855) and go R on this, to a X-tracks and turn L and shortly L again at another X-tracks (704/851). Past a house, on BW, **keep SA, to a lane** at the end (708/ 840) **and turn L,** over the cattle grid. Follow this for 1.2km (0.75m) to a X-crds (716/846) and turn R to Bromsden farm, **and keep SA alongside of black barn** (as drive bears L into the farm) **on a permissive BW, ST, DH.**

❸ Keep SA at the bottom, for 0.3km (0.2m) then turn L through a single gate at X-tracks (718/838). Steep UH, and keep SA at the top, through the woods along the obvious track. **Keep SA** when you see a FP sign pointing L, **to a fork** and marker post (green National Trust arrows, but no BW signs) **and bear L.** Feint track, along LHS of woods, through a single gate (BW sign on other side) and keep SA, to a rd and turn L on this, to a junction (732/845).

❹ Turn R on the tarmac BW, becoming gravel, past houses, and follow the BW into the wood, along a ST. **Keep SA/L on this ST,** which then steepens DH, alongside garden fences, **to a rd and turn L to the** (Fair Mile) **rd** (751/838). **Turn R** on the rough track before and alongside the rd, into Henley. Go SA at first roundabout, then R at the 2and (Kings rd), UH, bearing L, SA at mini roundabout, to a X-rds by the town hall (SA) (759/826).

❺ Turn L (one way system) to centre of Henley, **and follow rd hard R,** then SA/L towards Peppard golf course. After 0.5km (0.3m), turn L on Pack & Prime Lane (Rotherfield Peppard 3m). **Follow the BW** (R) **and keep SA on this ST,** DH then UH, **for 2.3km** (1.4m) **to a rd and turn R on this,** then shortly L on restricted ByW (730/821).

❻ Keep SA at a X-tracks then shortly L through a single gate on a BW (722/819). Follow this, exit the wood, bears R; then turn L past the farm buidling, DT, UH. Bear L at the farm, to the rd (716/805) and **turn R** on the rd and keep SA, past a pub, to a X-rds and go SA on Stoke Row rd, and just after/at a X-rds (704/813) (by a bus stop on the R), turn R on a ST, into the trees, on Peppard Common.

❼ There are a couple of tracks you could take, (twisty L in trees, or fast open on R) DH, to the bottom left corner and on obvious track, to a rd (706/818). Cross the rd to the BW, but use the ST on the RHS of the woods, which rejoins the BW later, past field, back into the woods, and take the first obvious track on the L (701/830), UH.

❽ DT, to the top and **go through the fence,** and go SA to the rd (drive to a house on R), and **go SA on the BW,** immediately bearing R at the ST fork, into Kingwood. Follow this to a drive (692/ 826) by Holly Tree Cottage and turn R on this or see the extension.

❾ When the drive ends **keep SA on the BW** (faded sign on silver gate to LHS of worksite), **keep R at fork,** to a DT and bear L here, on the stony DT, DH, to a rd (694/839).
9A Turn R on the rd, UH, to Highmoor Cross, **keep L,** to the B481 rd and turn L on this rd, then shortly R by the Dog and Duck **on a restricted ByW** (701/848).

❿ SA, to a X-crds (been here before) **and retrace your earlier tyre tracks,** by keeping SA, bearing R past Merrimoles, then keep L on DT, then R on ST, over main rd, SA, then L at X-tracks (709/864). To rd and R then L, **back on Old Kiln Road to the start** (702/868).

SHORT RIDE
10.7KM (6.6M) 235 metres of climbing

❶ Keep SA on Old Kiln rd, and take the 1st L, and keep SA on a private rd to Soundess House & Farm. Bear R at the end, on a DT, BW, DH, and keep R on this BW, past a house, to a rd (720/877). Turn R on the rd, for 1.3km (0.8m) then **L on the Oxfordshire Way** (726/870), steep UH. 0.65km (0.4m) to the top and turn R (723/ 876) on a ST BW, (fast) 1.6km (1m), to a DT at bottom (735/867).

❷ Keep SA to the rd and turn R on this, 0.8km (0.5m) into Middle Assendon, and take 2and rd on R (White Lane) (738 /858). UH for 1.2km (0.75m) and shortly after rd on R, keep SA on a BW as the rd bears L (727/854). **Keep SA** on this track, for 2.8km (1.7m) across a field, into the woods, over minor rd, on drive, past houses/Catslip **to a T-J with a minor rd** and turn R, then immediately **L** (705/ 868), back on Old Kiln Road, to the start (702/868).

* Can also be used as another extension.

EXTENSION
+10.5KM (6.5M) 125 metres climbing

❶ Go SA on the BW to L of the cottage, DH, to a rd and go SA on Hazel Grove BW, and keep SA on the BW, nice ST. At a rd bear R, over this and pick up the BW again, bearing R, to another rd and go SA, to another rd and go SA again. After 0.5km (0.3m) and turn R (north) at the end of the fence, by big house, on a DT, BW (669/806).

❷ Follow this, bearing R to a rd and turn L on the rd, and keep SA, then R at a fork, then R on a BW, just past the farm (667/817). Follow the BW, bearing L (674/ 827) to a rd and go SA/L on this, to a T-J in Checkendon (666/ 833). Turn R for 0.5km (0.3m) then turn R on a BW (669/ 837) in the dip and keep SA on this to a rd (677/829).

❸ Turn L and follow this rd, UH, to a T-J in Stoke Row (682/840) and turn R. After 0.7km (0.45m) (shortly after entering trees and going DH) turn R on a BW (689/840) and keep R at a fork after 0.75km (0.45m) (past wooden posts). Keep R at another fork, over a DT to a T-J (694/ 831) and turn L, and keep L, DH on a DT, to a rd (694/839) and rejoin the main route at no.9A.

GETTING THERE: Park on Old Kiln road (by the bus stop) in Nettlebed village, off the A4130 (702/868), or Maidensgrove Nature Reserve car park (721/878) on the short ride. Railway station at Henley (miss out Nettlebed to make a 22KM (13.75M) 340 metre ride.

ACCOMMOATION: White Hart (gasto pub) in Nettlebed 01491 641245. Lots of choice in Henley, inc Swiss Farm campsite on 573 419. Henley T.I. on 578034.

BIKE SHOPS: Very basic spares at AutoLex in Henley on 01491 577 720. Saddle Saffari in Marlow, AW Cycles in Caversham (Reading), Mountain high in Pangbourne, and Rides on Air in Wallingford.

REFRESHMENTS: A small shop & a pub in Nettlebed, lots in Henley, pubs in Rotherfield Greys, Sonning Common, and Highmoor. Also in Middle Assendon on short ride, and pubs and small shops in Checkendon and Stoke Row on the extension.

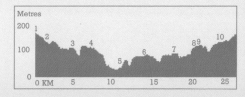

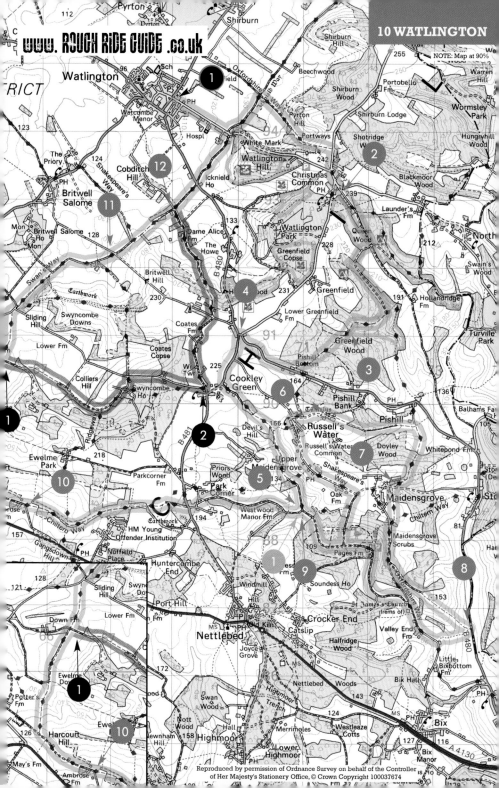

39KM (24M) 770 metres of climbing

❶ START. Turn R out of the car park, to a T-J (pub on L) and go L/SA on the rd for **0.9km** (0.55m) turn L on a BW (SU 698/940). After **0.8km** (0.5m) turn R on a ST rd (703/946), and keep SA on the grass, as the track bears R, UH, to a rd (715/ 937). Go R on this for **0.5km** (0.3m), then L on a rd, then immediately bear R on a rd/drive (715/931).

❷ Keep SA, for **1km** (0.6m) becomes rough DT in woods, and turn R (720/923) past a barrier, into the open on a DT, and follow this, past another barrier, bearing L, fast DH, to multiple X-tracks in a clearing (722/913) and turn R, following the white 'CW' arrows, UH, then L, DH, to a (DT) X-tracks at the bottom (716/910).

❸ Go SA, UH to a X-tracks at the top and keep SA, DH then UH to a clearing, and keep R. Follow the white 'CW20' arrows through the wood, DH to Grove fm (708/905) and go through the gates to a rd (701/910). Turn R on the rd, UH, L to a T-J with the B481 rd (700/910).

❹ Turn L on the rd for **0.8km** (0.5m), then L after the first house, on a gravel BW (697/902). Keep SA, becoming a ST between the trees, keeping R at fork after **1.1km** (0.7m) for **0.85m** to a T-J (710/884) and go L or see the shortcut

❺ After **1km** (0.6m) turn L at a X-tracks on a steep UH (716/879), for **1km** (0.6m) to a rd (718/887). Turn L on the rd for **1.6km** (1m), to Russell's water then R on a gravel track just past a pond (708/898). Onto the common and keep SA on the garvel DT to a farm (713/898).

❻ SA through a farm , then ST for **2km** (1.25m) to a T-J (end of trees) (727/897). Turn R, on the LHS of the field, DH to a X-tracks at bottom and go SA, steep UH, and bear L, follow white 'OW PS17' arrows to a rd (724/888).

❼ Go SA, UH on the BW (Oxfordshire cycleway & white arrows), exiting the woods and across the field, between the houses to a farm and turn R, then immediately L at a grass triangle (on the cycle track). After **0.55km** (0.35m) bear L at a fork (723/877), (SW33), and follow this for **1.6km** (1m), DH to a DT, at the bottom (735/867).

❽ Turn R on the DT, UH in the field, then back DH, bearing to the R of a house, to a rd (731/865) and go R on the rd. After **1.6km** (1m), keep SA (Nature Reserve on L) (721/877) becoming off-road. Keep SA on this for **1.4km** (0.85m) to a T-J (709/884) (here earlier) now bear L.

❾ Bear to the R of the farm, UH to a minor rd and bear L to a T-J with another rd (693/885). Turn R on rd for **0.1km** then L on BW (opposite house) and keep SA, DH on the ST for **2.75km** (1.7m). Exit the trees and bear R to a concrete track and turn R on this, past some houses.

❿ Alongside the field for **1.3km** (0.8m) to the top (near a clump of trees on the R) and turn R on a feint BW (easy to miss) (658/891). DH, and keep SA on the DT for **1km** (0.6m) to a minor rd (663/906) and go SA or see extension. Through a field to a rd (665/914) and turn R on this, then immediately L/SA, as rd bears sharp R, on the (Swans Way) BW.

⓫ Keep SA on BW for **1.9km** (1.2m) to a rd (681/922) and go SA, (the nice ST on RHS in the trees along here is a FP). **1.3km** (0.8m) to some X-tracks with a concrete track (690/929) and keep SA to B480 rd.

⓬ Go SA (Icknield way) for another **1km** (0.6m) to a rd (698/940) and turn L on this, DH (came up this at the start). After **0.55m** keep SA, as rd bears L, by the pub, and shortly L back into the car park (691/944).

SHORTCUT:
-12.9KM (8M) -300 metres of climbing

❶ Turn R at the T-J (710/884) and rejoin main route, which returns to this T-J on the track to the L, at no.13.

EXTENSION:
+3KM (1.85M) +75 metres of climbing

❶ Turn R on the rd, UH for **0.3km** (0.2m) then turn L on a BW (666/905) by the brick pillars, along the field edge, joining a DT and bear R on this. **1.1km** (0.7m) to a church and bear R, then L, UH, to a rd T-J (683/903). Turn R on this rd for **1.2km** (0.75m) to a (grass triangle) T-J (695/902) and turn L on the rd (FP) and follow this.

❷ Keep R by the farm, to a rd (696/913) and go SA (Woods farm - pig sign). After **0.15km** (0.1m) turn R on a BW (into the trees), DH, keep SA on the main track. Becomes a drive and keep SA, to a X-tracks (690/929) and turn R on a concrete track, and rejoin the main route at no.12.

GETTING THERE: Watlington is on the B4009, just 3 miles south junction 6 of the M40. Follow the signs to the (free) car park, down Hill road (690/944) or there is another (free) car park at Christmas Common (708/936). The nearest railway station is at Henley-on-Thames 5km/3m away. Go north-west on the A4130 to Lower Assendon, then R on the B480 (Stoner Valley) for 2.4km/1.5m, and join the route at no.8.

ACCOMMODATION: B&B's in Pishill on: 01491 638601 or another on: 638351, Camping in Henley on: 01491 573419, YHA in Bradenham (nr High Wycombe) on: 0870 7705714, Henley T.I. on: 01491 578034

BIKE SHOP: Rides on Air in Wallingford: 01491 836289

REFRESHMENTS: Shops, pubs, etc in Watlington, and pubs in Pishill, Maidensgrove, Christmas Common, and Nuffield.

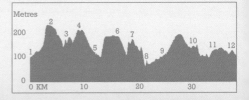

31.7KM (19.7M) 800 metres of climbing

❶ START. NOTE: For a technical DH to start, see the highlighted red route, otherwise **head south** (Fox pub on L) on the rd to a X-rds, at the end of the common (SU 753/937). Turn R on Grays lane, and keep SA to the end of the lane, then bear L into the woods **on a BW, going DH,** to the bottom (751/919) and bear L on the BW.

❷ 0.8km (0.5m) to a rd (757/916) and turn L on the rd, UH, to a T-J. Turn L on the rd for 0.15km (0.1m) then turn R on a concrete track behind the school (758/927).

❸ Go DH on a concrete track for 0.3km (0.2m) then turn R on a ST BW, through the woods (760/930), as the concrete track deteriorates. Exit the woods and **go over a DT,** to a T-J and turn R on this, for 2.1km (1.3m) to a rd (774/918). Turn L on the rd for 0.7km (0.45m) then turn R on a BW (773/924) into woods, UH, **to the top,** (781/925).

❹ Bear R, DH to a T-J and keep R/SA on a good track, past a house and out of the woods, through a gate and to the rd (781/912). Turn L on the rd for 0.7km (0.45m) to a fork and bear R (Frieth). After 0.25km (0.15m) turn L into the woods (789/912), past a fence and **steep UH on a BW.** After 0.5km (0.3m) turn R at the X-tracks (signposted as a FP, but it is a BW) (791/908).

❺ After 1m bear L onto the rd (780/902) and turn L, UH on this for 1.45km (0.9m) to a T-J (793/902) and go R on Parmoor lane. Follow this rd for 0.9km (0.55) then **bear R off the rd,** towards the convent (795/895) and keep SA, on a fast ST DH to a rd. Turn L on the rd, DH to a T-J (776/899) (there is a pub to the right).

❻ Go L/SA on the rd for 1.6km (1m) to a X-rds (777/888) and turn R (Vineyard) on a **steep, long UH. To the corner of a rd** (758/888) and turn R/SA or see extension 1.
6A After 0.5km (0.3m) go R on a BW at Kimble farm (753/889) and follow it, **becomes a ST,** DH. Follow main track keeping R for 2.4km (1.5m) **to a rd** at bottom (764/904).

❼ Turn L on the rd for 0.15km (0.1m) then R on a BW (763/904) along the edge of a field, through a gate and SA through a tunnel of trees. Join a drive, past a school, **to a T-J in Turville** village (768/911). The Bull & Butcher pub is on the R. Turn L on the rd, out of the village and immediately L on a BW (765/912), which bears R, then L after 0.8km (0.5m), UH into the woods.

❽ Go UH to a T-J at the top (755/910) and turn L on a DT, through a gate (brick wall opposite) and turn R on a drive. To a T-J with a rd and go SA/R for 0.5km (0.3m) and keep R at the fork (by some houses) (748/908). After 0.4km (0.25m) at the X-rds (744/910), and go SA/R on the BW (between the rd's going SA and R.

❾ Through the trees, into clearing **bearing L across the common** area going DH on the BW just past Turville Heath farm. 0.9km (0.55m) to a rd (747/919). Turn R on this rd for 0.25km (0.15m) then go into the woods (750/919), and L on the BW (you came down earlier), back UH, to the start (751/941), or see extension 2.

EXTENSION 1:
+7.6KM (4.7M) 190 metres of climbing

❶ Turn L on the rd for 1.4km (0.85m) then turn L on a BW, by the Roundhouse, as the rd bears R (758/875).

❷ Follow the BW for 2.4km (1.5m) (watch for tree roots as you exit the woods, DH), **and go DH on the grass,** to a DT (775/861).

❸ Turn L on the DT, UH, following the BW to Upper woodend farm (758/883). Bear L, to the rd and turn R on this (been on this rd earlier) to the T-J and turn L, and rejoin the main route at no.6A (758/888).

EXTENSION 2:
+3.8KM (2.4M) 110 metres of climbing

Ⓐ Just after crossing Ibstone common, **shortly after you enter the woods, turn L at the BW X-tracks** (749/938) - haven't been down hee before. Keep L on the BW, DH through the woods, on a fun, technical ST. Bears hard R half way down, then **out into the open and a T-J** (745/941) at the bottom.

Ⓑ Turn R and follow this trail for 1km (0.65m) to a multiple junction (744/949) of driveways, and turn R on a BW, going steep UH, into the woods. To a rd at the top (749/951) and turn R, for 1km (0.65m), **back to the car** (749/942).

GETTING THERE: This ride starts from Ibstone, which is just west of High Wycombe. Exit the M40 at junction 5 and head south for 2 miles into Ibstone and park in one of the lay-by's on the right, near the Fox pub (751/941).

ACCOMMODATION: B&B's in Pishill on: 01491 638351 and 638601 (near the Crown pub). Camping at Henley on: 01491 573419 or www.swissfarmcamping.co.uk. YHA in Bradenham (nr High Wycombe) on: 0870 7705714 or call High Wycombe T.I. on: 01494 421892 for more options.

BIKE SHOPS: Saddle Safari in Marlow: 01628 477020 or Cycle Care in High Wycombe: 01494 447908

REFRESHMENTS: This ride is blessed with lots of great country pubs. There is one conveniently situatein Ibstone at the start/end and some lovely ones on the route in Fingest, Freith, Skirmitt, and Turville.

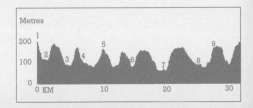

www. ROUGH RiDE GUiDE .co.uk

32.1KM (20M) 630 metres of climbing

1 START. At the northern end of car park, go to and over the rd onto a DT. DH, for 1.3km (0.8m) then R on the Ridgeway BW (SU 720/ 968), just past a house. Under the M40 and keep SA on this BW, over 3 rds, for 6.8km (4.2m) to a fork (SP 770/011), or see the extension 1.

2 Bear R, past a house, on the Ridgeway ByW for 1.45km (0.9m) to a rd (783/011). Turn R on this for 0.3km (0.2m) then keep SA through a gate, on a BW, at a lay-by. Keep SA for 1.5km (0.95m) to the end of the field (SU 795/996) and bear R then L (effectively SA) alongside a hedge.

3 Joining a good track and keep SA, past a farm, to a rd (803/983). Turn R on rd, UH, into Bedlow, to a T-J and turn L them immediately R on a BW. DH, to a rd and turn L then immediately R on a BW and keep L, UH, to a rd (791/964).

4 Turn L, or see the shortcut, on the rd for 0.65km (0.4m) then turn R on a BW, DH, into some woods for 0.4km (0.25m) to a T-J (794/957). Turn L and follow this for 1.6km (1m), joining a good track, keep SA on this, to the A40 rd. Cross this rd onto Chipps Hill rd opposite, and keep R and immediately turn R on a BW (806/942).

5 UH, for 2.35km (1.45m), past a farm, to a rd (785/ 945) and turn R on this rd, UH, for 0.8km (0.5m) to the A40 rd . Turn R on this rd for 0.25km (0.15m) then L on Water End rd (788/952). 1.3km (0.8m) to a T-J and turn R for 0.5km (0.3m) then L on a BW (Pophleys) (781/966).

6 Bear R, between houses, DH, to a rd and turn L on this, bearing R, UH. Keep SA on track (C14) when the rd ends (772/978). Follow the white (RA35) arrows along the edge of the wood, for 1.3km (0.8m) to a (BW) T-J (761/982) and turn L.

7 0.8km (0.5m), UH then DH, to a T-J with a DT (760/ 975) and turn R on this. Keep L for 1.6km (1m), heading towards a radar mast, to a rd and turn L on this, to a T-J with the A40 rd. Turn L on this then immediately R on another rd and follow this for 2.5km (1.55m) (or see extension 2) back to the car park (on the L) (726/958).

EXTENSION 1:
+1.6km (1M) +80 metres of climbing

1 After 5.3km (3.3m) at 3rd rd (SP 760/002), turn R on it UH, 0.8km (0.5m) to T-J and go L (Chinnor hill) for 0.4km (0.25m) then bear L on Hill Top Lane (SU 764/997).

2 Keep SA to a car park, and go SA on a BW to the L of the car park, (not L on a BW, DH). Go between 3 wooden posts, DH (the higher track on the L is rooty), to a T-J with the Ridgeway, at the bottom, and turn R to a fork and rejoin the main route at no.2.

EXTENSION 2:
+3KM (1.9M) +90 metres of climbing

A Just over the M40, when the barrier ends, turn L on a ST BW, back on yourself (SU 737/963). Into Wormsley Estateand keep SA on the main track, DH, following white arrows for 1.6km (1m) to a drive at the bottom (744/949).

B Turn R, and R again, past Wellground farm, UH, and keep SA past the 2 Vicar's farms, to a rd (729/961), and go L on this, 0.45km (0.3m) to the car park (L) (726/958).

SHORTCUT:
-7.4KM (4.6M) -130 metres of climbing

1 Turn R on the rd and follow this, keeping L, for 1.1km (0.7m), then turn R, off the rd, onto a BW (Pophleys) (SU 781/966) and rejoin the main route at no.6.

GETTING THERE: The ride starts from the (free) 'Cowleaze Wood Sculpture Trail' car park near Stokenchurch. Exit the M40 at juntion 5 and head north west on the A40, after 0.6m turn L on another rd (SP Sculpture Trail) for 1.5m and the car park is on the left (725/955). There is a train station in Chinnor.

ACCOMMODATION: B&B in Radnage on: 01494 484835 and Great Kimble (Bernard Arms) on: 01844 346172, YHA in Bradenham (nr High Wyco-mbe) on: 0870 7705714, High Wycombe T.I. 01494 421892

BIKE SHOPS: Cycle Care in High Wycombe (225 Desborough Road) on tel: 01494 447908.

REFRESHMENTS: Pubs in Chinnor (& shops) Bledlow Ridge, Piddington, Beacon Bottom, The City.

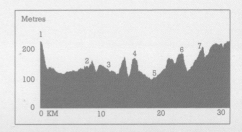

35.8KM (22.2M) 785 metres of climbing

❶ START. Follow the track at the back (NW) corner of the car park and shortly along here turn R on the Icknield Way Path (SP 822/037) or see the alternative (red) start. If yoy reach a gate and clearing you've gone too far. Follow this BW to a junction (829/ 036) and turn L, DH and shortly turn R then L (easy to miss as you race down as the FP goes SA) and follow this BW, to a rd (833/045).

❷ Go over the rd and turn immediately sharp R on a BW. **2A** Runs parallel with the rd for 0.4km (0.25m) then bearing L into woods, to some X-tracks and keep SA and follow the BW to a rd (843/046). Cross the rd and turn L on a BW (parallel to the rd), bearing R along the field edge, emerging by a farm.

❸ Go SA (to the LHS of the farm), UH on the Ridgeway for 0.3km (0.2m) to a X-tracks (848/050) and turn R. To a rd after 0.7km (0.45m) and go SA (L at T-J, then R through green gates) on the BW , and turn R by a house, to the 'Rising sun' pub (857/040). Turn L on the (Chilterns way) BW, DH for 0.9km (0.55m), to a DT at the edge of the woods (860/047) and turn R (not on the DT).

❹ UH, in the woods, to the top and go R along the edge of the woods for 1.2km (0.75m) to a rd (869/036). Go SA on a BW and SA at a X-tracks. After 0.9km (0.55m) as you exit the wood, (878/030) bear L at a fork, DH in a tunnel of trees, then under a tunnel, to a main rd (884/033).

❺ Turn R on the rd for 0.3km (0.2m), then L on Leather lane (The Lee) (888/029). 1.3km (0.8m), UH to a T-J (898/033) and turn L (The Lee), for 0.8km (0.5m) and bear L at the grass triangle (897/038) and follow the blue cycle signs, for 2.25km (1.4m) at a T-J in Kingsash (888/ 056) and turn R (or turn L then R to Concord House, DH, and bear L on BW, fun DH to Ridgeway and -4.2km).

❻ 0.5km (0.3m) bear L/SA on a BW for 1km (0.65m) and join rd keeping SA/L on this for 1.3km (0.8m), then turn L on a BW (Ridgeway) (897/ 074) as rd drops DH. Follow the BW, DH, bearing R, for 2.25km (1.4m) to a T-J (882/ 064) and go R on the DT for 1.1km (0.7m) to X-rds (874/071) and turn L to the A413 roundabout (872/068).

❼ Take the 2and exit (Little London), for 0.5m then bear R on the IWP at Smalldene farm. 1.1km (0.7m) to a T-J (861/056) and turn R (leaving the IWP) and follow this BW

SA, for 1.45km (0.9m) then bears R (853/067). Keep on the LHS, becoming DH, exiting at a rd (863/074).

❽ Turn L on the rd for 1.6km (1m) then turn L (south) on a BW (847/ 071) opposite gold club, and follow this SA to a rd. Turn L, then very shortly R on the first (lower) BW (846/ 056), for 0.7km (0.45m) to a X-tracks (848/050) been here before. Turn R, DH, and retrace your tyre marks back to the rd crossing (833/045), but don't cross the road.

❾ Bear R and follow the BW DH, to the A4010 rd (822/ 053) and turn sharp L (south) on the BW. To a X-rds and go SA and keep SA to a T-J at the end (818/040) (or turn L after 0.55km (0.35m) on the VERY steep Ridgeway BW, to the top - also a great DH), and turn L, steep UH, back to the car park (823/036).

ALTERNATIVE START

❶ Keep SA, through a gate and clearing, following the BW (IWP), through single gate, steep DH. To a DT and turn R (821/042) and follow this BW to a rd (826/045) by a (good) pub. Turn R, UH, for 0.7km (0.45m) then join the BW just after the car park (833/045), and rejoin at no.2A.

EASY RIDE
10.2KM (6.4M) & 160 meters climbing

① Turn L on the rd for 1km (0.6m) then R on a BW (830/ 029) at the start of the woods. Keep SA on this BW for 1km (0.6m) exit the wood to a track and go L on this to a rd (827/019). Go SA/L on the rd for 0.55km (0.35m) then R on a BW (SP Redland End on L) into woods (833/018).

② 0.5km (0.3m) to a DT, exit the wood and go L on a BW (830/014) past Lily farm, 1km (0.6m) to X-tracks and go L (836/007), between the hedges. 0.8km (0.5m) to a X-rds (843/011) and go SA/L on a rd (844/ 011) for 0.4km (0.25m) to a T-J and go R then L at grass triangle.

③ After 1km (0.6m) turn L on a drive (Hampden House and church) (851/022), and keep SA on the BW when the drive ends. 2.25km (1.4m) to a (BW) X-tracks (by a hut) and go SA, bearing L, to a rd and turn R on this, for 0.25km (0.15m) then R into the car park (824/035).

• **NOTE:** Add another 5.9km (3.7m) and 180 metres of climbing, by riding the first little loop of the main route.

GETTING THERE: This ride starts from a (free) height restricted car park just outside the town of Princes Risborough. Exit the A4010 on Peters Lane (northern edge of Princes/Monks Risborough) and follow this uphill for 0.8m and the car park is on your left (824/035). Railway station in Princes Risborough.

ACCOMMODATION: B&B in Little Hampden (at the Rising Sun pub) on: 01494 488393/488360, B&B in Wendover on: 01296 696759, YHA in Bradenham (nr High Wycombe) on: 0870 7705714, and Princes Risborough TI: 01844 274795.

BIKE SHOPS: Bolton Bikes & Tandems (behind Lloyds), in Princes Risborough on: 01844 345949

REFRESHMENTS: Pubs at Little Hampden, The Lee, Lee Gate, and variou in Wendover, and Princes Risborough. Pub in Great Hampden on short ride.

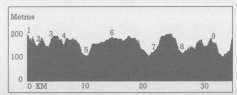

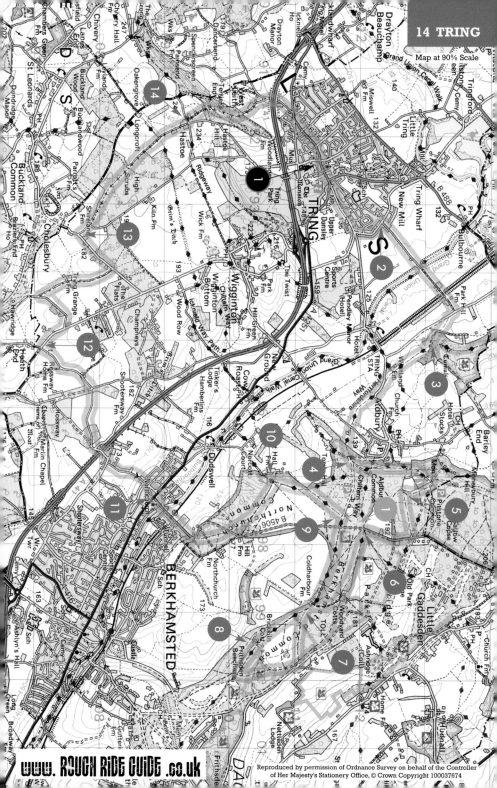

31.6 (19.6M) 460 metres of climbing

1 START. Exit the car park and go L (on High St), to a roundabout (by Robin Hood pub) and go SA, then immediately bear L on Station rd. SA for 0.8km (0.5m) to X-rd (SP 934/123) and go L on Grove rd (934/119) for 0.3m then turn R on Marshcroft lane (932/123).

2 Keep SA for 1.8km (1.1m) over the canal and railway (look out for the dogs), to a rd (945/134). Turn R. on the rd then very shortly turn L on a BW, keeping SA at a DT, just inside the woods, to a X-tracks (951/129) and go SA on the Ridgeway (RW).

3 0.65km (0.4m) to a X-tracks and go SA (leave RW) to a rd and bear L on this. After 0.3km (0.2m) keep SA on a BW, as rd bears L, to a rd (962/118), and go SA on a BW. UH, at the top bear L to a rd, and go R on this for 0.25km (0.15m) then L on a BW (969/119).

4 Keep SA over a DT (drive), bearing R to a (feint) X-tracks (968/121) and keep SA, UH, on a DT. After 0.55km (0.35m) go SA at the X-tracks, then shortly bear R at a fork (968/128). UH to the top by the monument, past the Visitor centre/cafe to the rd and turn R into the car park (970/131).

5 Exit the car park at the far left on a good track, for 0.5m to some X-tracks (972/126) and turn L on the BW. 0.7km (0.45m) to a rd (978/128), and turn R on the main rd, for 0.8km (0.5m) then L on the (Chiltern way) BW (977/120), or see the shortcut.

6 SA for 1km (0.65m) to a drive (987/117), and bear R on this, for 0.4km (0.25m) UH, to the top (988/112) and go L, through the trees, on a BW as the drive bears R. After 0.15km (0.1m) bear L at a fork into the open and bear L along edge of the woods/common.

7 0.5km (0.3m) to the DT on the other side near a rd (997/110) , and turn R on the DT for 0.4km (0.25m) then bear L on a BW, into the woods, as the DT bears R. Go SA at the 1st X-tracks to another X-tracks (999/101) and turn R, for 0.55km (0.35m) to a gravel DT.

8 Turn R on the DT, then shortly SA/L (to the RHS of the house), on a BW, into the trees, leaving the DT as

it bears R. SA for 1km (0.6m) to a fork (been here earlier) and bear L. To a drive (988/112) and turn L on this and keep SA on the BW, to a rd (977/116), and go SA on the rd opposite.

9 After 0.15km (0.1m) go L on a BW (975/117), for 0.8km (0.5m) and go L at a feint X-tracks (971/112), keeping along the LHS of the woods. 0.55km (0.35m) to a X-tracks (970/106), and go L, exit trees, and bear R, along the edge of the common (woods on the RHS).

10 After 0.65km (0.4m) (dips DH then UH) bear R, on grassy DT, BW (975/103), before the car park. Keep SA to a rd, and go SA on a BW, and keep SA at some X-tracks, over a drive to a rd (979/0945) and turn L/SA on this, DH, over a bridge, to a T-J.

11 Turn R then shortly L (972/088) on Darrs lane (by the One stop shop), steep UH for 1km (0.6m), to the top. Turn R on the rd, bearing L over the A41 (966/080) and keep L at the fork, and follow this rd for 2km (1.25m) to some X-rds (951/071) and turn R.

12 0.5km (0.3m) to a fork (948/074) and bear L (Cholesbury), for 0.7km (0.45m) then R on a BW. Keep R at Tring Grange farm, to a rd (939/081) and go L on this for 0.7km (0.45m) then R on Kiln lane (934/076).

13 After 0.15km (0.1m) keep SA/L on a ByW as rd bears R, and keep SA for 1.4m to a X-rds. Turn L then immediately R on a ByW at a grass triangle (917/093).

14 Keep to the RHS of the house, DH on the ByW (Hastoe Lane, becoming West lieth lane), to a rd T-J (914/105). Turn R under a bridge, to the main B4635 rd, and turn R on this, back into Tring (921/113), and car park on the L.

SHORTCUT:

-5.6KM (3.5M) -60 metres of climbing

1 Keep SA on the rd, for another 0.4km (0.25m) then turn R on a rd (977/116) and rejoin the route at no 9.

GETTING THERE: Tring is on the A41, between Hemel hempstead and Aylesbury. There is a car park in the centre of Tring. Tring train Station, just outside of Tring, near Aldbury.

ACCOMMODATION: B&B's in Tring on: 01442 826638 and 828327. YHA Ivinghoe on: 0870 7705884 and Silver Birch campiste by Ivinghoe on 01296 668348. Tring T.I. on: 01442 823347

BIKE SHOPS: Mountain Mania Cycles in Tring: 01442 822458.

REFRESHMENTS: Lots of choice in Tring (Tringfellows cafe comes recommended) and in Aldbury. There is a cafe at Pitstone common, a shop in Berkhamsted.

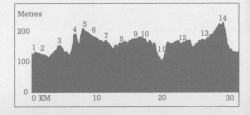

DIY ROUTE

Woburn Sands has lots of trails throughout the woods, and we have marked some trails on the map, but to get the best out of it you really need a local to guide you - see right.

If you really have to / want to go at it alone and explore it for yourself, Stockgrove Park makes a good starting point as there is a nice cafe, a few trails and it can be linked to Woburn pretty easily via the Greensand Ridge Walk.

These are just some of the trails to find*:

1. Roller coaster

2. Golf course trail

3. Ditches single track

4. Tight n Spikey

5. New Bridge single track

6. Field Edge single track

7. Sandy Lane single track

8. Trippy Trucker Trail

9. Roundhouse steps

* Please note that different people have different names for the trails.

There are also some downhills and jumps over, near the Woburn village side of the woods.

Some tracks are out of bounds to cyclists.

•NOTE: There is an annual charge (currently £11) to ride in the woods - see www.greensandtrust.org/pdfs/permit_app_bike_07.pdf or pay the warden if and when you see him.

CYCLONE MTB CLUB

Website: www.cyclonemountainbikingclub.co.uk

The Cyclone MTB club has been established for over 10 years and rides weekly at Aspley Guise woods based in Woburn Sands.

Club rides are every Sunday, and meet at the top of Church Road at 10 and 11am, and on the first Tuesday of the month in The Swan in (the middle of) Woburn Sands.

Rides are fun, sociable events, with people being happy to wait and lend a hand, or show you some technical challenging trails. They are keen to introduce new people to the club, so go and ride with the club and see how you get one with them.

Rides are guided by a MIAS Level 2 qualified Club Comittee member, who can also offer instruction and advice if required. They are a friendly bunch, with riders of all abilities from beginners through to advanced, and will be happy to hear from you, so contact them and find out more.

WOBURN CRANKERS

Website: www.woburncrankers.com

They say they're not really a club, but more a bunch of guys in various states of health and fitness who enjoy riding their mountain and road bikes.

Rides normally start / meet at Stockgrove Country Park, on Sundays at 8(ish), with an hours ride, then meeting others either at the runners car park by the church at Bow Brickhill at 9am, returning to Stockgrove Country Park for 11.30 and a post ride snack in the cafe.

Check out the message section on their website for more information.

GETTING THERE: Aspley Guise woods is based in Woburn Sands, on the south-east edge of Milton Keynes. Exit the M1 at junction 13 and aim for Woburn Sands. There is parking in the centre of the woods (take note the closing times), or go to Stockgrove Country Park car park (918/294), off the A5, near Heath and Reach. There are train stations close by in Bow Brickhill and Woburn Sands.

BIKE SHOPS: Phil Corley Cycles in Milton Keynes on 01908 311424, Roy Pink Cycles in Newport Pagnell on 01908 21068, Cycle Connections in Leighton Buzzard on 01525 852400.

ACCOMMODATION: Fir Tree Hotel on 01908 582127, Station Hotel on 582495 and Greens Hotel on 512400, all in Woburn Sands. B&B's at The Old Stables on 01908 281340 and Woodley Farmhouse on 582242, both in Woburn Sands. YHA in Limton Keynes on 0870 770 5716. Milton Keynes T.I. on 01908 558300.

REFRESHMENTS: Pubs in Woburn Sands and a pub in Bow Brickhill, and good cafe in Stockgrove Country Park.

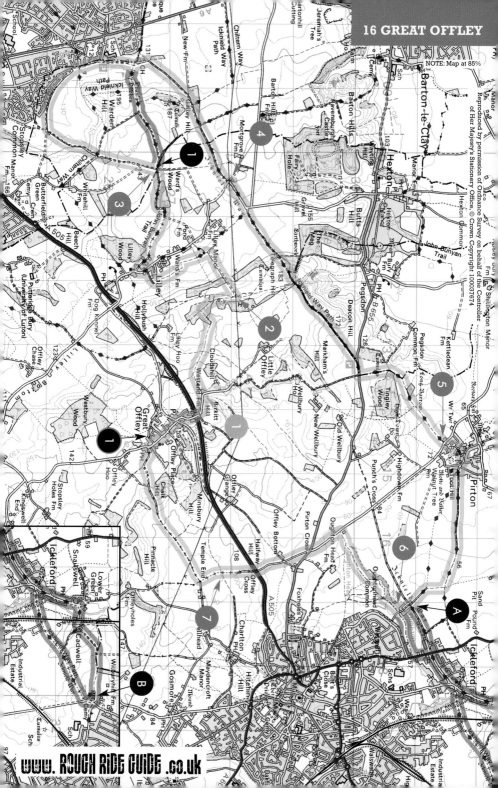

NOTE: Map at 85%

Reproduced by permission of Ordnance Survey on behalf of the Controller of Her Majesty's Stationery Office, © Crown Copyright 100037674

www. ROUGH RIDE GUIDE .co.uk

29.8KM (18.5M) 380 metres of climbing

① START. Back to the X-rds by the Greene Man pub (TL 141/271) and go SA on School lane. 0.3km (0.2m) after crossing the A505, keep SA/L on a BW as the rd bears R or see the shortcut. After 0.3km (0.2m) bear R at the fork (134/273), keep SA at a X-tracks after 0.4km (0.25m), through a field, then bearing L around the back of some trees. UH, in the woods to a T-J (124/275) and go R for 0.65km (0.4m) to a junction under elec pylons (122/280).

② Turn L on the DT, DH for 0.8km (0.5m) then turn L on a BW as the DT turns sharp R (115/276). Keep SA for 1km (0.65m) through the gates to a X-tracks (in a clearing and FP only SA) and turn R (120/267). To a rd and turn L for 0.15km (0.1m) then turn R on West Street (118/264), which becomes a ByW. Follow this (John Bunyan trail) for 1.95km (1.2m) (bearing to the LHS of the woods), DH to some X-tracks (102/268) and turn L, or see extension 1.

③ UH for 1km (0.6m) to a X-tracks and keep SA, back DH towards the houses (Luton). 1km (0.6m) to a X-tracks at the end of field (097/250), turn R on a track going on the RHS of houses. 2.4km (1.5m(to some X-tracks just past the golf clubhouse (086/266) and turn R (after Tee no.10), on the Icknield way. 3A Keep SA on the main track for 2.6km (1.6m) to a rd and go SA/L on the rd.

④ After 0.5km (0.3m) keep SA, back onto the Icknield way path, as the rd bears sharp L (109/282). Keep SA on the Icknield way for 3.2km (2m) (L at a fork after 0.8km/0.5m by the Telegraph hill sign) to a rd (132/300). Turn R on the rd for 0.25km (0.15m) then L on a BW (134/301). Keep SA on this for 2km (1.25m) to Pirton village (145/314) and go SA on the (Crab tree lane) rd opposite.

⑤ Past Motte & Bailey pub to a T-J (High St) opposite the Fox pub and go R (147/317). 0.15km (0.1m) to a T-J and go SA through a gate on Icknield way BW. After 1.85km (1.15m) bear R (167/314), staying on good track (Hitchin 1.6km/1m), to a grass triangle, and bear R then L through a white gate, or see extension 2. Keep SA, over the river then immediately R on a BW by the river (171/307).

⑥ Nice ST for about 1.6km (1m), by the end of the woods bear R then L (SA) to a rd (158/297). Turn L on the rd for 0.55km (0.35m) to a X-rds and go SA on Wibbly Wobbly lane. 1km (0.6m) to a dual carriageway (165/284) and go SA on a ByW opposite, SA for 0.5km (0.3m) to a X-rds.

⑦ Go SA, for another 0.4km (0.25m) to another X-tracks, turn R on a R.O.W. (166/275), under the electricity pylons and keep SA for 1.6km (1m) (become a good track). To a fork and bear R, emerging by the Red Lion pub (146/266). Turn R (on the High street), then shortly L on Salisbury lane then R on Clarion Close, back to the car park (143/267).

SHORTCUT:

-14KM (8.7M) -200 metres of climbing

① Keep R on the rd for another 0.55km (0.35m) and go R at the fork (136/280) by the houses (New Wellbury). Follow this for 2.35km (1.45m) to a rd (134/300) and go SA on the (Icknield way path) BW, and rejoin the main route at no.8. NOTE: This can also be used in reverse, to reduce the ride by 8km/5m & 100 meters of climbing.

EXTENSION 1:

-2.25KM (1.4M) but uses a steep DH

① Keep SA for 0.15km then bear L at the fork (100/268), and keep SA for 1.6km (1m) (down a steep hill) to X-tracks (086/264). Turn R, past the golf club house and then turn R again past Tee no.10, and rejoin the route at no.3A.

EXTENSION 2:

+7.9KM (4.9M) +65 metres of climbing

Ⓐ Turn L on (Icknield way) lane for 0.8km (0.5m) to the A600 rd and go SA (Turnpike lane). SA at the roundabout, (Arlesey) then under a railway bridge. After 0.15km turn R on a BW (188/324) for 0.15km then L through Cadwell farm (189/323). After 0.5km (0.3m) turn R at a fork (192/326) UH for 0.8km (0.5m) into a wood by the picnic area.

Ⓑ Bearing R, for 0.15km then R on a ByW (200/324) DH, past the railway, back to Arlesey rd in Ickleford (183/316). Turn L, to the roundabout then SA/R on Turnpike lane for 0.5km (0.3m) to the main (A600) rd (177/312). Turn L on this rd for 0.3km (0.2m) then turn R on a BW (178/309) just over a bridge. After 0.8km (0.5m) alongside the river rejoin the main route at no.4 (171/307).

GETTING THERE: Great Offley is between Luton and Hitchin, on the A505, which runs between the A1 and M1. Turn onto the High Street (by the Green man pub) then right on Gosling rd, then left on Clarion Close, then left again into the car park (143/267). Railway station in Hitchin (shown on the map).

ACCOMMODATION: B&B in Lilley (at the Lilly Arms) on: 01462 768371, B&B in Charlton (at the Greyhound pub) on: 01462 440989, Hotel (at the Lord Lister) in Hitchin on: 01462 432712, Luton T.I. on: 01582 401579

BIKE SHOP: C J Frost & Sons in Hitchin: 01462 434433

REFRESHMENTS: 4 pubs & a post office shop in Great Offley. More pubs in Lilley and Pirton, Ickleford and Letchworth on extension 2. The pub in Charlton (just off the route, near the end) is nice.

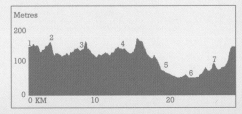

www. ROUGH RIDE GUIDE .co.uk

33KM (20.5M) 425 meters of climbing

❶ START. Head (east) away from car park entrance on the wide track. After 2.6km (1.6m) turn R immediately after crossing a bridge, following the horseshoe signs to a rd (309/ 116). Turn L on the rd, UH for 0.15km (0.1m) then R on a BW (signposted as a FP) for 1.2km (0.75m) to a driveway (302/104) by a farmhouse.

❷ Turn L on the drive, which bears R, and follow it for 1km (0.6m) past a quarry, bear L over a bridge, to a rd (298/ 096). Go SA (slight L) on a BW, joining a drive (301/089) and keep SA to a rd. Turn L on the rd for 0.4km (0.25m) then L on Bucks Alley (BW no.3) (294/080) or see shortcut 1.

❸ 1.3km (0.8m) (down and up a dip) to a T-J and turn R, then after 0.65km (0.4m) turn L on White stubbs lane (302/070). 0.65km (0.4m), along this turn L on the Chain Walk ByW (308/071) into the woods or see shortcut 2.

❹ Keep SA to a rd (311/083) and turn R on it for 1.4km (0.85m) to the Farmers Boy pub and turn L on a BW (Fanshaws lane) (322/080). 1.4km (0.85m) to a rd (325/093) and turn R on this for 0.3km (0.2m) then bear L on a ByW shortly after a farm and keep SA for 0.8km (0.5m) through a farm, becoming a rd.

❺ After 0.15km (0.1m) keep SA/R on the BW as the rd bears L (335/085) and follow this for 1.45km (0.9m) (DH then UH). Joins a drive by some houses and turn R on the BW, after Bramble wood house, before a rd (343/075).

❻ Follow this through the woods to a DT and turn L on this, to a rd (340/070). Turn R on the rd for about 1km (0.6m) then R on the permissive path next to the rd. Keep L through the car park (with picnic tables), staying close to the rd, to a fork and bear L to the rd (324/070).

❼ Turn R on the rd for 0.25km (0.15m), then L on a BW (322/072) for 0.8km (0.5m) to a rd (317/067). Turn R on the rd for 0.65km (0.4m) then turn L on a ByW (not signposted), opposite Claypits farm (311/068).

❽ Keep SA for 2.35km (1.45m) becomes tarmac, and passes houses and a hotel, to a rd (302/049) and go R on this (past a pub). After 0.15km (0.1m) bear L off the rd on New park rd (LHS of Nelito's restaurant) (300/050). Follow this DT, becoming off-road, for 1.6km (1m) bearing sharp R, and keep SA on the DT to the rd or see the extension.

❾ Turn L on the rd for 0.1km then R (284/058) on Cucumber lane for 1.8km (1.1m) to a fork in the rd (276/072).

❿ Turn R on Berkhamsted Lane, for 1.45km (0.9m) then turn L on a BW, through the white gates (288/076).

⓫ Follow this for 1km (0.6m) then take the 2and R (just before the metal gates to the farm) (282/084). 1.45km (0.9m) to a rd (282/098) and go SA on the BW (Letty Green) for 1km (0.65m) then turn L on a DT (unsuitable for motors) (284/108) by the green, as the rd bears R

⓬ Follow this for 0.9km (0.55m) close to the duel carriageway then turn R on the permissive path (276/108). 0.25km (0.15m) to a T-J and turn R (276/109) on a good wide track. Follow this for 1km (0.6m) back to the car park (285/111) on your L.

SHORTCUT 1:

-20KM (12.5M) 270 meters of climbing

① Keep SA, 0.3km (0.2m) into the village, to a fork and bear R on Berhamsted lane, for 0.4km (0.25m) and turn R on a BW through the white gates (288/076), and rejoin the route at no.11.

SHORTCUT 2:

-10KM (6.2M) -130 meters of climbing

Ⓐ Keep SA on the rd for another 0.4km (0.25m) then turn R (opposite Claypits farm) (311/068) on a ByW (no signpost), and rejoin the main route at no.8.

EXTENSION:

+4KM (2.5M) +50 meters of climbing

❶ Shortly after the DT turns hard R, turn L on a BW, for 2.2km (1.35m) past a farm, to a rd (265/056) (Grubbs lane opposite). Turn R on this rd, but use the path along the side for your safety.

❷ After 1.4km (0.85) then turn R on a (Tylers Causeway) BW (270/067) and follow this for 1.45km (0.9m) to a rd (280/060). Turn L on this for 1.3km (0.8m) to a fork (276/072) and rejoin the main route at no.10.

GETTING THERE: The ride starts from the free Green Way car park (with height restriction), in Letty Green (between Welwyn Garden City and Hertford). Leave the A414 at the Cole Green turning, then turn right to Letty Green, then left just after the Cowpar Arms pub, before going under a bridge, to the car park and picnic area (285/111). Train station on the route at Bayford, and Hertford and Welwyn Garden City, which a cycletrack (part of the route) links together.

ACCOMMODATION: B&B in Cole Green on: 01707 333225, and Newgate Street (farm) on: 01707 872509. YHA in Lee Valley park, in Cheshunt on tel: 0870 7706118. Camping & Caravanning nr Hertford on tel: 01992 586696. Hertford T.I. on tel: 01992 584322.

BIKE SHOPS: Marshalls in Welwyn: 01707 393322 & Hertford on: 01992 503868

REFRESHMENTS: Cowpar Arms at the start, Farmers Boy at Brickendon, Coach & Horses or Crown at Newgate Street, and Greene Man at Little Berkhamsted.

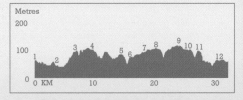

37.2KM (23.1M) 260 metres climbing
(includes 5.8km/3.5m loop on the red route)

TOP TIP: There is lots to do / ride in Rowney Warren Woods, so make sure you have lots of energy for here - if that means taking shortest route from the train station, or driving, so be it.

❶ START. From St Johns railway station in Bedford, (TL 049/490), follow Ampthill St (north side and parallel to the A6) to a big rounabout and take 1st L on Kingsway (one-way). Keep in the R hand lane at the end and turn R on Cauldwell Street, to the end, then L on St Mary's St.

❷ Turn R, crossing the rd just before the bridge on a cycle path (no.51) and follow this alongside the river. Follow the cycle path signs for Willington, and R into the village and follow the rd past the pub, to the A603 rd (115/496).

❸ Go SA on Wood lane and keep SA past the farm, UH on a stone DT, becoming a grassy DT at the elec. pylon, to a rd (134/478). Turn R on this rd and follow it to a T-J. Go SA on the DT towards the farm, bearing L on the BW before the farm.

❹ Follow this ST, becoming a better DT for 1.35km (0.85m) then turn R over a small wooden plank bridge, leaving the DT, staying on the Greensand Ridge Walk. Bumpy track, gets better, to a rd (112/444). NOTE: Seasonal permissive ROW (for walkers only!?) through Warden Woods SA.

❺ Turn L on the rd, then first R (SP Haynes), to a T-J and turn R and keep R, to a X-rds with the A600 rd (116/416). Go L, then R on a forest DT, into Rowney Warren Wood, and just down here is the Freeride area and signs for the red and blue XC routes and ride whatever takes your fancy.

❻ When you are ready to go, join the John Bunyan Trail BW (good surfaced farm track) that runs along the southern edge of the woods. UH, then DH, through a gate, to a rd. Go L on this for 0.45km (0.25m) then R on a grassy DT BW (101/412).

❼ To a rd (103/418) and go L, to a T-J and turn R, then immediately L on North Lane (097/420) and keep SA. Becomes a DT, DH, through a farm, to a rd and turn R then L on the John Bunyan Trail BW, (079/442) gravel track, becomes grassy DT.

❽ Over a cattle grid and bear L at the barn, following the DT, becoming tarmac. Follow this to a T-J (051/468), and turn R. Keep SA on High St (dead end rd) by the Red Lion pub, to a roundabout and go SA (SP Town centre) on Elstow rd.

❾ Follow this to a T-J (053/489) and go L, over a bridge, to a roundabout and go L and back along Ampthill St (north side / parallel to the Ampthill Rd / A6), back to St Johns train station (049/490).

ROWNEY WARREN WOODS

2 way-marked Cross Country trails (both of which start and end at the main car park), a Freeride area (off the main access road at north end of the woods) a Dual Slalom, 4X course, dirt jumps, some Northshore obstacles and some downhill runs.

Blue Route: 4km/2.5m (generally) easy route which is suitable for beginners, that maily follows the wider forest trails.

Red Route: 5.6km/3.5m more demanding cross country route with more single track, and a number of short steep climbs and descents. There is also an optional technical loop through the Freeride Area, offering additional drops and jumps.

The Freeride, Dual Slalom, etc are situated at the far northern end of Rowney Warren. To get there follow the Blue XC route from the Sandy Lane car park, to the main access road at the northern end of the wood. Following the Blue XC Route down the access road, the Dual Slalom Area is on your right.

• NOTE: The XC trails are open public access, but membership is required at weekends and bank holidays for the Freeride and Dual Slalom areas. Day Tickets are available on the day.

For more information see www.bedsfattrax.org

TOP TIP: Arlesey train station is closer to Rowney Warren Wood, so you may well want to go from here. From the staion (189/378), head west on the A507 to a roundabout and turn R (Henlow), then L at the next roundabout. Through Clifton, and Shefford to the B658 and go L on this to the A600, and go SA on the BW to the south west edge of the woods (122/401).

GETTING THERE: By car, head for Shefford, where the A507 and A600 roads cross, then go north on the A600, to the woods. There is the main car park on Sandy Lane (123/404), or parking by the X-rds (115/416) at the northern end of the wood (by the Freeride area). By train, Arlesey station is closer (8km/5m each way), but St Johns in Bedford (18.6km /11.6m there & 13km/8.1m back) offers more off-road.

ACCOMMODATION: Lots in Bedford. B&B in Shefford on 01462 811353. No YHA or campsite nearby. Bedford T.I. on: 01234 215226.

BIKE SHOPS : Halfords Bike Hut in Bedford on: 01234 262212.

REFRESHMENTS: Lots in Bedford. Pubs in Willington and Deadman's Cross, good snack van at the main Rowney Warren Wood car park, and a pub in Haynes.

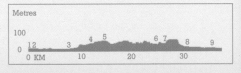

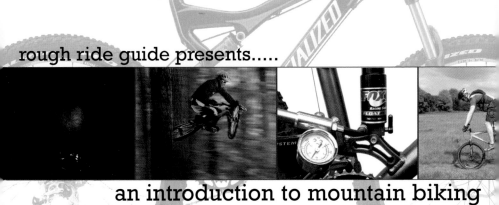

brought to you

by

ROUGH RIDE GUIDE